Secrets, Truths, & Whispers

Lessons from a Good, Hard Life

Tony Garcia

Distribution by Bublish, Inc.

ISBN: 978-1-64704-216-5

This book is printed on acid-free paper.
Printed in the United States of America

To my children: Jennifer, Ryan, Melissa, and Kyle.

You taught me the greatest lesson of all: how to love.

Contents

a note from G

at the beginning of this process, I was a reluctant writer, simply urged on by loved ones, friends, followers, strangers, and the occasional passerby. I did not see the wonder in my words. They were but my own random musings. But many shared with me how my simple verses spoke directly to them. The more I wrote, the more I was urged to put my words into a book. *Wanna Know a Truth?* was born from those who had unknowingly pushed me well beyond my comfort zone. It was not an easy process. I was extremely critical of my own work. I was far from a professional writer. Who was I to have a published book? And yet, three years later, *Wanna Know a Truth?* continues to find an audience. I could not have imagined the reach it would have, nor how it would change me.

A year later, I would go on to create *Whispers from My Heart.* I felt more comfortable with this work. I had grown as a writer, was more willing to take chances, less stuck in the flow and form I had tied myself to in my initial work. During this time, my life was changing, and it was reflected in those passages. Pieces penned by a man truly in love, words formed by a man feeling completely broken. It was a daunting process, to speak of things I barely dared to whisper. It was a frightening and difficult journey from the light to the darkness to the light once again. Few knew of the emptiness, the loss, the injury in my heart. *Whispers from My Heart* was a helpful step in the healing. The words came from a bone-raw place in me. And yet they still spoke of an unwavering hope.

Through it all, I continued to write. I continued to grow, change, heal, move forward. I continued to find my way along. It has been two years now since *Whispers from My Heart* was published. I have captured those years and my journey in this newest work. My writing has continued to evolve. I have made some changes to the format of my previous two publications. I think this is the book I always hoped I would write.

I am much more at peace with my gift: the ability to simply say what so many are feeling. I am much more at peace with my life. A heart that is healed. A purpose-filled life. A gentle, humble man still hoping to make a difference. What follows are secrets I have uncovered, truths I have come to know, whispers I listen to, and lessons that this good, hard life has provided me.

~G

part one: secrets

discovering what lies buried within

All the secrets of the world worth knowing are hiding in plain sight.
—Robin Sloan

This, my only resolution. Live.

Fully live

Hopefully

Gratefully

Peacefully

Truly live

True of word

True of deed

True of heart

Simply live

Simply me

Simply aware

Simply present

Deeply live

Deeply pray

Deeply love

Deeply believe

Fearlessly live

Less fearful of failure

Less fearful of change

Less fearful of not knowing

This, my only resolution. Fully, truly, simply, deeply, fearlessly . . . live.

The path to success requires
Faith of heart
Discipline of habit
Elimination of excuses

The path to success may
Leave bruises and scars
Try to break you
Take you beyond comfort

The path to success will
Tap into your fears
Challenge your commitment
Question your resolve

The path to success is
Open to all willing to try
Seldom a straight line
Likely an uphill climb

The path to success is not
Measurable in numerical terms
The same for everyone
Impossible to navigate

The path to success has
Few rest stops
Many dead ends
Turns you won't see coming

The path to success has no
Shortcuts
Easy routes
ETA

The path to success
Stretches out before you
Whispering your name
Inviting you to dance.

I quit.

I quit listening to the voices of fear and doubt
So I could finally begin hearing the whispers from my heart

I quit giving energy to what I could not change
So I could finally begin changing what I can

I quit running from my shadows and fears
So I could finally begin chasing my dreams

I quit seeking excuses for why I shouldn't
So I could finally begin living without regret

I quit focusing on what I thought I was missing
So I could finally begin appreciating what I have

I quit comparing my journey to another's
So I could finally begin enjoying where I stand

I quit playing small for the sake of another
So I could finally begin growing into myself

I quit viewing myself through the lens of others
So I could finally begin to see the real me

I quit worrying about what others think of me
So I could finally begin to become who I am to be

I quit.

So I could finally begin.

I continue to struggle.

I continue to struggle
For I am willing to try once more

I continue to struggle
For I am bound by my humanness

I continue to struggle
For I seek the wild horizons

I continue to struggle
For I reach what is beyond my comfort

I continue to struggle
For I challenge the notion of impossible

I continue to struggle
For I do not concede to failure

I continue to struggle
For I choose the path uncharted

I continue to struggle
For I run undaunted into the storm

I continue to struggle
For I insist upon raising my own bar

I continue to struggle
For I chase a distant dream

I continue to struggle
For I refuse to surrender to "good enough"

I continue to struggle
For I desire to feel goose bumps and butterflies

I continue to struggle.

For I know, within the struggle, a warrior is forged.

I redefined myself when I changed how I defined what I wanted for my life.

Courage: trembling yet still leaping

Discipline: not "should" or "could" or "would," but rather, "will"

Gratitude: being thankful, even for the storm

Happiness: wanting what you have > having what you want

Hope: setting the alarm clock

Humility: allowing your actions to whisper your name

Joy: just dance, for it doesn't matter if everyone or no one is watching

Love: caring for yourself the way you care for those you care about

Peace: being where your feet are

Perseverance: give up giving up

Power: controlling your controllables

Resilience: trusting more, worrying less

Strength: finding a way when weakness is all you know

Success: the attempt that follows the most recent failure

Life: redefined.

I am becoming.

I am becoming beautifully stronger
The scars signal not a weakness, but an unwavering strength

I am becoming beautifully kinder
The words I now whisper to myself feel a lot like "I love you"

I am becoming beautifully grateful
The simple act of inhale-exhale is reason enough to give thanks

I am becoming beautifully patient
The rush to arrive has been replaced by the calm of accepting where I am

I am becoming beautifully enlightened
The darkness, no matter its depth, cannot envelope the light placed within me

I am becoming beautifully carved
The weathered brow and deepening lines are living proof of one who smiled, even in the face of the storm

I am becoming beautifully real
The layers of my yesterdays have peeled away, revealing who I am today

I am becoming, beautifully.

I wanted to go back to a moment in time
When I could have forgiven myself

I wanted to go back to a moment in time
When I could have told myself, "You will be okay"

I wanted to go back to a moment in time
When I could have chosen a different path

I wanted to go back to a moment in time
When I could have started again

I wanted to go back to a moment in time
When I could have dared greatly

I wanted to go back to a moment in time
When I could have been a little stronger, a little braver

I wanted to go back to a moment in time
When I could have picked myself up off the floor

I wanted to go back to a moment in time
When I could have listened to my heart whisper, "You are meant for more than this"

I wanted to go back to a moment in time
When I could have loved myself a little bit more

I wanted to go back to a moment in time
When I realized that now is a moment in time.

I wanted to be more.

I wanted to be happier. So I decided to smile and laugh and dance and celebrate living. I began to chase dreams, goose bumps, and light instead of people and things. I stopped grieving over what I do not have and found joy in all I do have.

I wanted to be more at peace. So I decided to quit defeating myself and to do more to develop myself. I began to take time away from the noise, the race, the worries. I stopped comparing myself to others and caring what they thought of me.

I wanted to be more grateful. So I decided to express my thanks for all that came my way. I began appreciating the lessons that hard times taught me. I stopped living from a place of trying to fulfill myself and moved to one of helping to fill the cups of others.

I wanted to be stronger. So I decided to address my weaknesses and shortcomings. I began to surrender my ego, realizing strength often requires seeking help. I stopped doubting my ability, my capacity, my resolve to achieve what I sought.

I wanted to be more loving. So I decided to allow my heart to heal its old wounds. I began to practice positive self-talk, to provide daily self-care, and to allow myself to be loved. I stopped searching for love and sought instead to become a living, breathing act of love.

I wanted to be more. So I decided to be more.

I was feeling devoid of hope
I am finding a light from within

I was left to wander alone
I am finding comfort in the company I now keep

I was so very lost
I am finding my way home

I was rushed and harried from the race
I am finding it is okay to slow my pace

I was convinced I was to blame
I am finding I need not own the faults of others

I was led to believe I was not worthy
I am finding the power to determine my own value

I was afraid to take the leap
I am finding confidence in the wings given to me

I was repeatedly knocked down
I am finding strength to stand again

I was bowed and broken
I am finding my way toward healing

I was too busy counting all that I don't have
I am finding that adding up my blessings leaves me little time for anything
else

I was
I am finding I am not what I once was.

I know you know the steps.

This is just a reminder.

1. Wake up: seriously . . . wake up!

2. Remember your reasons: you are worth them

3. Get up: one more time

4. Deep breath: you can do this

5. Tuck yourself in: keep your faith, hopes, and dreams tucked really close

6. Lace 'em up: tie them tight so you won't come undone

7. Head up, eyes forward: these, the directions you are heading

8. Shoulders back: stand tall, shrink from nothing—be it a task, a challenge, your light

9. Lean forward: engage your core (beliefs)

10. Launch yourself: with confidence, courage, and conviction, you can go everywhere

11. Keep breathing: the difficult always fades—always

12. Fight for your finish: do not surrender the vision

I know you know the steps.

This is just a reminder of how you face this life.

Keep the faith
Lose the doubt

Raise your words
Lower your voice

Hold onto hope
Let go of fear

Lead by example
Follow your heart

Speak more gently
Listen less distractedly

Be slow to anger
Be quick to forgive

Give more of yourself
Take less from others

Fall always forward
Get up never discouraged

Sow joy
Reap goose bumps

If there was to be one guiding principle by which I attempt to live my life, it would be as simple as this: opposites attract.

Worry less about what others think about you
They do not think about you as often as you think they do

Worry less about your greatest fears
They have rarely ever come to pass

Worry less about the challenges between you and your end goal
They exist only to help ensure you become strong enough to finish

Worry less about the things you cannot control
They are not as important as the things within your control

Worry less about the numbers you obsess over
They can never measure your worth or value

Worry less about the tomorrows yet to arrive
They are unpromised gifts that distract from the present that is today

Worry less about the plans of others
They have a race to run that is not yours

"Worry less": two words life often whispers.
They all too often go unheard.

For you. For a friend. For one in need.

Dear Me,

I miss you. I miss the you who was so brave. How I loved your courage to try, to leap, to dare, to dance. Once, you did not fear.

I miss you. I miss the you who shined your brilliant light. How I loved your hues, your shades, your true colors. Once, you did not hide.

I miss you. I miss the you who believed. How I loved your belief in the possibilities, in dreams coming true, in the existence of miracles. Once, you did not doubt.

I miss you. I miss the you who persevered. How I loved your grit, your determination, the warrior in you. Once, you did not quit.

I miss you. I miss the you who was free. How I loved your unbridled joy, your unfurled wings, your untamed heart. Once, you did not cage yourself.

I miss you. Today, I shall set out to find that you, and when I do, I shall love you.

Like I once did.

Love,

Me

Grant yourself at least one word: "yes"

Permit yourself at least two words: "I can"

Tell yourself at least three words: "I love you"

Promise yourself at least four words: "I will not quit"

Remind yourself of at least five words: "I deserve my own love"

Brave yourself with at least six words: "I will not fear the difficult"

Commit yourself to at least seven words: "I am going to do what's necessary"

Owe yourself at least eight words: "I alone am responsible for my emotional well-being"

Trust yourself with at least nine words: "I am strong enough to handle come what may"

Speak to yourself, at the very least, like you believe in yourself.

Until I am strong again
I may rise a little slower
But I will find a way to my feet

Until I am strong again
I may slow my pace
But I will keep moving forward

Until I am strong again
I may need to rest a bit more
But I will not give up the fight

Until I am strong again
I may have to ask for help
But I will not see it as weakness

Until I am strong again
I may focus too much on my pain
But I will remember the wounds are healing

Until I am strong again
I may not feel okay in the moment
But I will get there in time

Until I am strong again
I may not have what it takes today
But I will show up again tomorrow

Until I am . . .
I may . . .
But I will . . . be strong again.

Again, today, you did it.

You put forth the good fight

You rose to your feet

You did not let the darkness win

You held onto a hope

You bested a demon

You believed enough to try

You moved closer to healing

You refused to surrender

You grew stronger

You made it beyond the struggle

You willed yourself better

You did not break

Again, today, you did it.

Tomorrow shall be no different.

Your challenge should challenge you.

Your challenge should challenge your thinking

Your challenge should challenge your way of doing business

Your challenge should challenge your belief

Your challenge should challenge your abilities

Your challenge should challenge your possibilities

Your challenge should challenge your complacencies

Your challenge should challenge your worn excuses

Your challenge should challenge your comfort zone

Your challenge should challenge your capacity to endure

Your challenge should challenge your willingness to continue

Your challenge should challenge your discipline

Your challenge should challenge you.

Do not fear when it does.

Things no one can ever take from you:

1. Your beautiful: for it is not determined by some random, arbitrary definition. Not a pop culture fashion statement. Not a "one day here, next day gone" thing. It is simply how you arrive.

2. Your worth: for it is not based on what's trending. Not related to fans or followers, likes or comments. Not ever a number. You are priceless. It has been indelibly established.

3. Your joy: for it does not depend on another. Not outside your locus of control. Not a whim or feeling. It is a conscious, intentional way of moving through your day.

4. Your power: for it is not something you must cling to. Not able to be wrested from you. Not based on size, stature, or position. It is found in the choices you make to be healthy, strong, better.

5. Your dance: for it is not choreographed by another. Not based on someone else's song. Not open for interpretation. It is an expression of the beauty, worth, joy, and power you possess.

Things no one can ever take from you.

Now that you know, I say to you, "Good morning, beautiful. Know your worth, express your joy, use your power for good, dance your dance."

Here's a thought.

Maybe you're not everyone's cup of tea
Because maybe you're just too hot to handle

Maybe you're not everyone's thumbs-up
Because maybe you're a whole handful

Maybe you're not everyone's MVP
Because maybe you're not into playing games

Maybe you're not everyone's "all that"
Because maybe you're enough just like this

Maybe you're not everyone's first chair
Because maybe you're the entire symphony

Maybe you're not everyone's rainbow
Because maybe you're the storm

Maybe you're not everyone's everything
Because maybe you're finally understanding you don't ever have to be

There's a thought.

I realized my path would not always be so difficult, so I went ahead, trusting it would get easier.

I realized my dream would not always be so distant, so I went ahead, knowing it would soon be within reach.

I realized my days would not always be so dark, so I went ahead, searching for the light to return.

I realized my fear would not always be so great, so I went ahead, refusing to bow to it.

I realized my wings would not always be so fragile, so I went ahead, allowing them to unfurl.

I realized my storm would not always be so torrential, so I went ahead, finding the rainbow within it.

I realized my heart would not always be so bruised, so I went ahead, feeling it slowly beginning to heal.

I realized my love would not always be so hard to accept, so I went ahead, giving it away unconditionally.

I realized my life would not always be, so I went ahead, making it as beautiful as I could.

Some look with their eyes and cannot see more than my physical limits

Some look with their love and see I am more than my body gives me credit for

Some look with their eyes and cannot see beyond the scars that have cut me open

Some look with their love and see the signs that remind them of my strength

Some look with their eyes and cannot see I am not my failings

Some look with their love and see all I have overcome to stand once again

Some look with their eyes and cannot see anything but my flaws

Some look with their love and see an imperfect masterpiece

Some look with their eyes and cannot see who I truly am

Some look with their love and see who I always hoped I would become.

Striving to be better
Striving once more
Striving for me

Giving to be better
Giving once more
Giving for me

Letting go to be better
Letting go once more
Letting go for me

Rising to be better
Rising once more
Rising for me

Searching to be better
Searching once more
Searching for me

Forgiving to be better
Forgiving once more
Forgiving for me

Healing to be better
Healing once more
Healing for me

Changing to be better
Changing once more
Changing for me

Loving to be better
Loving once more
Loving for me

Living to be better
Living once more
Living for me

To be better. Once more. For me.

The invitation.

I invite you to simply breathe.

To merely inhale and exhale. Nothing more. Simply feel the rise and fall of your chest. To pause. To collect yourself. To realize nothing sustains life more than the simple act of breath-taking. Be still, my friend. Just breathe. From this place, all things can be faced.

I invite you to conquer only this moment.

Stay here. Be present. This singular moment, and all that it can possibly hold, is not larger than you. It is when you drag forward all the moments that have passed, or worry about those yet to come, that this moment seems overwhelming. Win these sixty seconds.

I invite you to nurture your inner child.

Speak to that little one. Grant her permission to be okay. Tell her you have always loved her. Tend to the wound with grace and kindness and forgiveness and love. It is time to heal. She is waiting to come home. Extend your own invitation.

I invite you to state your affirmations.

It may seem brash, perhaps too bold, but you are permitted to speak your truth. "I am calm. I am strong. I am okay." You need never shy away from your own light. "I am beautiful. I am worthy. I am loved." In speaking your truth, the universe shall greet you as such.

I invite you to rejoice in being you.

Well, will you look at you? Oh my. You are a magnificent, glorious, beautiful being! In all the universe, you are uniquely created. That makes you a miracle. And better still, the odds of being you are one in seven billion! How lucky you are! Celebrate your gifts, your light, your amazing self.

I invite you to invite yourself.

This one fragile, precious, amazing life you have been given is calling. Invite yourself. To know joy. To feel goose bumps. To dance. To wander aimlessly. To see your beauty. To dive into the deep end. To unfurl. To endlessly and breathlessly love yourself.

You have been invited.

When I thought no one could possibly save me from going under once more, someone extended me a lifeline.

When I thought no one cared to know of the hopes and dreams I held closest, someone said, "Tell me of such things."

When I thought no one dared brave the demons that haunted me, someone stood unafraid to face them.

When I thought no one was strong enough to pull me from the depths of the enveloping darkness, someone grabbed hold of me.

When I thought no one wanted to hear the quiet whispers of a kind and gentle spirit, someone leaned in closer to listen.

When I thought no one would be able see the beautiful soul behind the scars, someone gazed upon me with wonder.

When I thought no one loved all my broken, scattered, and missing pieces, someone loved me hard enough to put me back together.

When I no longer thought of myself as no one, it turns out I was someone enough.

Ways to simplify your life:

1. Declutter your thoughts: Your brain is on overload, filled with so much clutter. The cannots, should nots, what ifs, negatives, fears, and excuses are all talking up too much space. Clear the brain cabinets. You need one thought up there: *I can do this.*

2. Unpack your bags: I sense that much of your fatigue and energy expenditure comes from carrying around all that useless baggage. But look at you hauling it around like a trophy. Time to put it on the curb. Nothing in there is of value.

3. Shorten your to-do list: Breathe, trust, be grateful, keep moving, seek joy, love hard. Imagine if you simply applied those principles to all facets of your life. I don't know much, but if this is what's on your get-done list, I'm pretty sure you're winning.

4. Turn down the noise: Crazy? Funny? Odd? Not sure which it is, but how you refuse to filter out all the white noise in your life is confounding. What other people say and think, the worn recording of your self-loathing, the whispers of doubt. Unplug the headphones.

5. Establish your nonnegotiables: Know very specifically what you are willing to accept in your life. Then do not stray from that place. When something does not have a place, clutter and baggage begin to take hold. If it does not add value to your life, do not invite it in.

6. Keep it simple: Stop making everything so complicated. Problem? Solve it. Need? Get it met. Wound? Tend to it. Question? Ask it. Dream? Go after it. Out of your control? Stop worrying about it. You are equipped with enough tools. Use them.

7. Have some perspective: It isn't the mountain you are tripping over; it's that darn crack in the sidewalk. Problems are not always as grand as we make them out to be. To most every situation you have faced, you have found a way. Remember that. And next time, pay closer attention, pick up your feet, or walk a different path.

Understanding my greater-thans.

Where I'm going > Where I've been

Times I've risen > Times I've been down

My hopes > My fears

My quiet confidence > The voice of doubt

The strength I possess > The burden I bear

The light within me > The darkness of the storm

A desire to leap > The trembling keeping me grounded

A faith that guides me > The unseen path

Lessons learned > Mistakes made

Blessings I've been given > Perceptions of what I am lacking

Human kindness inherent in me > Any evil that humans can learn

The belief in who I am > What others think of me

My unwavering love > The heartbreaks I have known

When I came to understand my greater-thans, I made a promise to myself: I will never view myself as less than ever again.

I am breathing slowly
Allowing myself to simply catch up to the moment

I am healing slowly
Allowing myself to mend stronger than what cut me

I am moving slowly
Allowing myself to step away from the noise and the chase

I am rising slowly
Allowing myself to whisper a prayer before standing once more

I am growing slowly
Allowing myself to fit comfortably into the me I am becoming

I am learning slowly
Allowing myself to absorb the lessons placed before me

I am climbing slowly
Allowing myself to acclimate to the new heights I have reached

I am changing slowly
Allowing myself to gradually let go of what is no longer meant for me

I am dancing slowly
Allowing myself to find a rhythm that sets my soul ablaze

I am recovering slowly
Allowing myself to give my heart time enough to close the wound

I am realizing slowly
I am allowed to go about this life at my very own pace.

Sometimes I wonder if dreams do come true

Sometimes I wonder if hard work really does pay off

Sometimes I wonder if nice guys don't have to finish last

Sometimes I wonder if all things really do happen for a reason

Sometimes I wonder if the struggle is worth it

Sometimes I wonder if the odds aren't always stacked against us

Sometimes I wonder where the road less traveled will lead

Sometimes I wonder if my best is good enough

Sometimes I wonder at the wonder of it all

Sometimes I no longer have to wonder.

I did not know I was strong
Until I stopped to help another stand

I did not know I was home
Until I allowed another to seek refuge in my arms

I did not know I was wealthy
Until I let another know how valuable they were to me

I did not know I was a light
Until I sat unafraid in another's darkness

I did not know I was a mirror
Until I showed another their beauty reflected in my eyes

I did not know I was a flame
Until I handed the torch over to another

I did not know I was gifted
Until I gave my love to another

I did not know who I was to become
Until I unknowingly permitted another to see all I am meant to be.

If you love me
Please let me fall
But do not leave me
When I am down

If you love me
Please let me fail
But do not give up on me
When I am still trying

If you love me
Please let me wander
But do not turn me away
When I long to return home

If you love me
Please let me struggle
But do not lose faith in me
When I am finding strength

If you love me
Please let me change
But do not treat me like a stranger
When I am newly unrecognizable

If you love me
Please let me break open
But do not try to fix me
When I am sorting out the pieces

If you love me
Please let me grow
But do not stop loving me
When I am fueled by your love.

Essentials for every journey:

1. Patience: Even if not at the expected arrival time, you will get there. Breathe.

2. Gratitude: If you must have an attitude, make it one of gratitude. Notice how everything changes.

3. Faith: If you believe, you believe. Nothing should cause this belief to fray or come undone.

4. Peace: Some see themselves as lost. Others see themselves as simply on a new path. One causes panic. The other brings comfort.

5. Fortitude: Courage. Grit. Spunk. Resilience. Call it what you want. But have some. Quit stopping short.

6. Openness: No matter how many times you take the trip, there are lessons to be learned. Be open to them. You do not know everything.

7. Compassion: You will meet many along the course of your travels. All are worthy of your humanity and kindness.

8. Confidence: It is okay to see yourself as a strong, capable, magnificent being. And to know that you are worthy of the destination.

Essentials for every day.

I did not come here to steal your spotlight
But to help you see the light in you

I did not come here to steal your thunder
But to encourage you to dance in the rain

I did not come here to steal your time
But to cheer for you as you rise above the moment

I did not come here to steal your mojo
But to be inspired by your discipline

I did not come here to steal your story
But to be awed by the next chapter you are writing

I did not come here to steal your dream
But to look with eyes wide open as you track down your unicorn

I did not come here to steal anything from you
But to simply let you know there is plenty for both you and me.

Things to remember when your world gets turned upside down:

1. You are strong enough to support yourself

2. It feels different, but you are still standing

3. Balance is more crucial than ever

4. If you fall, you will land on your feet

5. With that in mind, trust the landing

6. You can still reach for the sky

7. Two words: fresh perspective

8. A solid base will keep you from collapsing

9. The key: tuck yourself in, stay grounded

10. Three points of contact remain: hope, faith, love

If you forget all that, remember this: you have the power to turn your world right side up again.

In the midst of your storm, take the following actions:

1. Brace yourself: even if it means taking a knee. There is strength to be found there.

2. Be still: You need not match the raging winds. Find your calm.

3. Seek higher ground: Stop going to the basement. Raise yourself up.

4. Take shelter: in that which is secure and steady. Hope, faith, family, friends, love.

5. Search for the rainbow: It will always appear. But you will not see it looking down.

6. Be your own umbrella: You are waterproof! Quit letting the storm make you believe you are not.

7. Learn to swim: or at least keep paddling. Whatever it takes to keep your head above water, do that.

8. Become the storm: For the love of humanity, fight back! You are strong enough.

9. Take comfort in knowing: The storm always passes. Always.

If you forget all that, remember this: You were made shrink-proof. The storm will never be larger than you.

A friendly reminder about being friendly:

1. Listen more: you will learn more

2. Extend an invitation: be the first to reach out

3. Use your manners: "please" and "thank you" still matter

4. Offer to help: even if it is just to hold the light

5. Lift your words: words hold power, so use yours for good

6. Be kind: meanness hurts even the strongest

7. Judge not: you do not know the entire story

8. Approach softly: everyone has a fragile place

9. Leave peacefully: others should want you to return

10. Let love guide your action: in all things, let love be the reason

A friendly reminder about being a good human.

How do you build a champion?

You begin by finding yourself a competitor. Someone who shows up and wants to do the work. Someone who finds a reason to keep trying. Someone who understands that excellence is not a switch you flip; rather, it is a way of doing business.

How do you build a champion?

You begin by finding yourself a humble servant. Someone who quietly leads by example. Someone who makes others want to be better. Someone who does not ask for the spotlight but does not fear the glare of the big moment.

How do you build a champion?

You begin by finding yourself a solitary figure. Someone who opts not to follow the crowd. Someone who, if needed, will stand alone for what is just and good and kind. Someone who dances unabashedly to their original song.

How do you build a champion?

You begin by finding yourself a warrior. Someone who stitches themselves together after every battle. Someone who is at peace with themselves. Someone who is beautifully scarred.

How do you build a champion?

You begin by finding yourself.

An open letter. To you. For you. Of you.

Dear You,

I know you wonder if anyone knows how strong you are becoming. In faith, in hope, in discipline.

I know you wonder if anyone realizes how far you have come to stand here today. Beyond the setbacks, the comfort, the status quo.

I know you wonder if anyone can see your wings unfurling. Fragile, yet strong. Untested, yet ready. Developing, yet beautiful.

I know you wonder if anyone appreciates how much you have grown. Larger than your fears, your excuses, your "cannot."

I know you wonder if anyone is paying attention to your story. A page turning, a chapter revised, a beautiful read.

I know you wonder if anyone is aware of the dreams you are chasing. Your wild horizons, your unicorn, your goose bumps.

I know you wonder if anyone has been witness to your uprising. The warrior, the champion, the storm you are becoming.

My friend, wonder no more. For I am amazed, inspired, and moved by the very wonder of you.

Love,

Me

How?

1. Work hard: Don't expect easy. In fact, be willing to accept the difficult.

2. Be disciplined: Make it what you do. Remove motivation, "want to," "feel like it," from the equation.

3. Unstick yourself: Break your tendencies. Old habits lead to yesterday's results.

4. Dare to risk failing: Expand your capacity. Try what you currently cannot do.

5. Invite feedback: Be open to growth. Watch, listen, adapt, improve.

6. Quit with the ing: whining, complaining, ranting, excuse-making, discounting. Quietly go about your business.

7. Challenge your nonsense: You believe some ridiculously false things about yourself. Change the lens through which you view yourself.

8. Defeat your tired: Identify what you are most weary of. Then set out to vanquish it.

9. Embrace the chase: Find your joy. If you are not having fun, you might be doing it wrong.

10. Understand the equation: input = output. What you invest will be returned.

How? How what?

How you succeed at anything.

I found the letter you began to yourself.

Dear _____,

There are some things I've been meaning to say to you. Some, I imagine, are long overdue. Some, not easily spoken but needing to be said.

I am sorry. I am sorry if I treated you as less than. Less than worthy, less than special, less than beautiful. I would not treat another as such. You deserve more than my second best. More than my less than.

I believe in you. I believe in your ability to overcome, to rise stronger, to make it to the light. I have seen you do it time and time again. And my belief deepens. I will no longer doubt you.

I want to be your friend. I want to put down the weapons of self-destruction, put down the chains, put down the put-downs. I want to treat you with kindness and grace and goodness. I want to be your best friend. Once again.

I am all in on you. I do not plan on giving up on you. No matter the struggle, no matter how long it takes, no matter what may come. I am all in. Completely sold on you.

I am amazed by you. If you only knew how I truly see you, feel about you, hope for you. You would stand a little taller, smile a little more, dream a little bigger. Oh, little one, you are an amazing being, just as you are.

I love you. I love all of you. Your broken and your beautiful. Your shadows and your light. Your history and your unwritten chapters. Your mystery and your magic. It is more than loving you; it is being in love with you.

There are some things I've been meaning to say to you. Some, overdue. Some, not easily spoken. And yet, now you know.

Love,

_____

Listen. Please.

I may not speak of my demons
It does not mean I am not waging a battle

I may not speak of my burdens
It does not mean the journey is easy

I may not speak of my fears
It does not mean the trembling has ceased

I may not speak of my loss
It does not mean I do not feel an emptiness

I may not speak of my troubles
It does not mean times are not hard

I may not speak of my darkness
It does not mean it has not arrived to envelope me

I may not speak of my heartache
It does not mean there is not pain

I may not speak of my brokenness
It does not mean I have not been shattered

I may not speak a word
It does not mean I cannot be heard

Please. Listen.

In our "do everything, be everything, accomplish everything" world, we lose sight of this simple fact: We need to focus only on the one thing that needs to be done. And so I made a promise to myself. I will look no further than the one thing set before me.

One rep at a time
I will get stronger

One mile at a time
I will run the race

One step at a time
I will climb my Everest

One obstacle at a time
I will overcome this challenge

One breath at a time
I will survive the difficult

One leap at a time
I will defeat what I fear

One prayer at a time
I will again rise from my knees

One piece at a time
I will stitch myself together

One day at a time
I will make it to the light

One word at a time
I will write my story

One act of kindness at a time
I will change the world

One heartbeat at a time
I will love and live this life

I made a promise to myself. I will look no further than the one thing set before me.

Discipline of thought
Stay positive
Show what you think by what you do
Practice mindfulness
Believe you can

Discipline of habit
Stay consistent
Show up
Practice addressing your weaknesses
Believe you are worth it

Discipline of action
Stay hungry
Show progress each day
Practice the mundane
Believe in your ability to change

Discipline of gratitude
Stay thankful
Show your gratitude
Practice counting your blessings
Believe in giving more than you take

Discipline of patience
Stay calm
Show you are ready
Practice being present
Believe in the process

Discipline of success
Stay humble
Show up no one
Practice, not perfection
Believe it is the only outcome

Discipline of the heart
Stay loving
Show all a loving grace
Practice forgiveness
Believe always in love.

These, the allies I keep near:

1. Discipline: the habit of maintaining my habits

2. Belief: a quiet, humble confidence that whispers, "I will"

3. Faith: an unwavering trust in the process

4. Perseverance: failing to yield when others would stop

5. Hope: knowing the storm will pass

6. Power: being responsible for my well-being

7. Patience: being exactly where my feet are

8. Gratitude: the practice of acceptance

9. Focus: eliminating the distractions

10. Love: living with my heart wide open

These, the allies who never fail me.

If ever words should fail me
I will quietly take your hand
And you will know, "I am here for you"

If ever words should fail me
I will quietly take your hand and kneel next to you
And you will know, "I keep you in my prayers"

If ever words should fail me
I will quietly take your hand and help you stand
And you will know, "I believe in your strength"

If ever words should fail me
I will quietly take your hand to walk beside you
And you will know, "You will never walk alone"

If ever words should fail me
I will quietly take your hand and lead you to the light
And you will know, "The darkness did not win"

If ever words should fail me
I will quietly take your hand gently to my lips
And you will know, "You are loved"

If ever words should fail me
I will quietly take your hand and place it on your beating heart
And you will know, "You are not broken"

If ever words should fail me
I will quietly take your hand and simply be your friend
And you will know all I ever hoped to say.

Dear Valentine,

Will you love me?

Not the ideal me. The imperfect, flawed, human me. The me who makes the same mistakes and doesn't always get it right. The me who tries and fails and tries and fails.

Will you love me?

Not the put-together me. The untucked, messy, coming-apart-at-the-seams me. The me who doesn't always have my junk in a pile. The me whose heart and life are held together with scar tissue, duct tape, and hope.

Will you love me?

Not the strong me. The on-bended-knees, bowed, weakened me. The me who needs help to stand. The me whose burdens and baggage often feel too great to overcome.

Will you love me?

Not the secure me. The worried, fear-riddled, anxious me. The me who sometimes doubts I am worthy of being loved. The me who fears love is simply waiting to once again make its exit.

Will you love me?

Not the filtered me. The blemished, scarred, 3 a.m. me. The me who has my ugly moments and ugly cries. The me whose demons awaken in the quiet hours just before the dawn.

Will you love me?

Not just the ideal, put-together, strong, secure, filtered me, but all of me. I ask this of you, because I have spent my life learning to love every piece of me.

And I have come to realize I deserve someone who will do the same.

Love, Me

Dear Child,

There are these things known as "social norms." They are unwritten rules of behavior that are considered acceptable or normal in a society. The problem is, given the current state of social media, you may be very confused about what is actually normal or acceptable behavior. And to further complicate matters, the big people in your life are adding to the confusion by the behavior they exhibit on social media.

I am not so sure they are setting the bar very high in regard to what is normal and acceptable. And while these are not necessarily the rules, I hope they might help you determine what you would like your standard to be.

It is completely normal and acceptable

1. To keep your private life private: it need not be everyone's business.

2. To keep your clothes on: dignity and modesty are not character defects.

3. To keep your circle small: not everyone who wants to be your friend is a friend.

4. To not rant, not comment, not like: not everything deserves your attention or energy.

5. To unfollow the crowd: you are not required to fit in or to be what's trending.

6. To remain positive: you do not need to go to the basement; it is okay to be a source of light.

7. To not seek attention: in a "look at me" world, it is okay to shine the light on someone else.

8. To celebrate others: another's success does not ever diminish yours.

9. To lose the filter: as you are beautiful enough, it is okay to just be real.

10. To take a break: not being "social" will likely allow you to be more social.

Perhaps I am merely old-fashioned and this new society has turned its back on me. Perhaps this new normal is here to stay.

Or maybe it is time we rethink our norms. And perhaps the change begins with you, little one.

I got honest with myself.

And it was not easy.

The lies I was telling myself kept me safe, comfortable, without risk, and free of failure.

"My excuse is valid," I proclaimed. It was a lie. Truth was "I wanted my crutch." If I held onto the lie, nothing needed to ever be risked. But the reality was nothing was ever gained. So I dropped my crutch and realized I am capable of running.

"I can't," I repeatedly said. It was a lie. Truth was "I won't." If I held onto the lie, failure was never an option. But the reality was I had made a choice to not even try. So I changed my "won't" to "will" and realized I cannot fail.

"This is impossible," I claimed. It was a lie. Truth was "This is difficult." If I held onto the lie, I was never put in a situation that made me uncomfortable. But the reality was I had slowly given up on things I truly wanted. So I faced the difficult and realized impossible is no longer my reality.

I got honest with myself.

And realized it was best thing I could have done.

If you want results
Have patience
Be disciplined
Do the work
If you want growth
Have a plan
Be open to change
Do new

If you want strength
Have faith
Be willing to address your weaknesses
Do one more
If you want freedom
Have courage
Be confident in your wings
Do your thing

If you want success
Have a target to aim for
Be unafraid of failure
Do something each day that moves you closer
If you want happiness
Have gratitude for little things
Be where your feet are
Do for others

If you want goose bumps
Have waking dreams
Be relentless in the pursuit of joy
Do life with arms wide open
If you want love
Have an open heart
Be aware of who is placed on your path
Do not be afraid to give

If you want for anything
Have space to receive it
Be humble when it arrives
Do not doubt you are worthy.

I am a little lost
But I will be okay
Faith is an internal compass

I am a little afraid
But I will be okay
Courage is just a deep breath away

I am a little worried
But I will be okay
Trust is a calming agent

I am a little weakened
But I will be okay
Hope is tomorrow's strength

I am a little fragile
But I will be okay
Friendship is bubble wrap

I am a little broken
But I will be okay
Love is a beautiful stitch

Little by little
I will be okay
For the big things I have in my life.

This is the story behind my single greatest excuse: I was too busy.

A darkness came to consume me
But I was too busy filling my lamp
With light, hope, and gratitude
And the darkness simply faded

A sorrow came to defeat me
But I was too busy filling my heart
With prayer, kindness, and faith
And the sorrow could not win

A failure came to define me
But I was too busy filling my pages
With lessons, growth, and once-mores
And the failure was barely a footnote

A fear came to paralyze me
But I was too busy filling my tank
With courage, trust, and belief
And the fear got left behind

A bitterness came to dine with me
But I was too busy filling my plate
With blessings, grace, and forgiveness
And the bitterness left no aftertaste

An emptiness came to settle in me
But I was too busy filling my life
With joy, goose bumps, and love
And the emptiness found no space

This is the moral of the story: if you are going to be too busy, make sure it is filling you, not draining you.

Knowledge that is good to have
Things to do with this knowledge

No one can steal your finish line
Do not worry if someone appears ahead of you

No one can walk in your shoes
Continue to follow the path meant for you

No one knows the price paid to become you
Never allow them to discount you

No one can speak lies that change your truths
Do not permit another's words to unravel you

No one owns the rights to your story
Decide what you want written in your pages

No one feels the tired in your bones and soul
Rest when you feel like resting

No one controls the key to your happiness
Try every single chamber until you find it

No one is capable of mind control
Do not let what others think alter your dreams

No one will ever be you
Be the priceless masterpiece that makes you

Knowledge is power
Now that you know, use it to do your things.

I arrived here today as a result of the principles and ideals that I have remained committed to throughout my journey.

These are the commitments I have made to myself—small, daily promises I work to keep.

You could say they are a part of my most rigorous and important training plan. My plan to simply be a better, stronger, more complete version of myself.

1. Be an act of kindness.

2. Raise my words, not my voice.

3. Give more than I can ever take.

4. Strive for measurable progress.

5. Know better, do better, be better.

6. Perpetually see and seek the positive.

7. Remain resolute in the face of difficulties.

8. Remain humble in moments of success.

9. Do not let others' minor actions cause major reactions in me.

10. Make a difference in the circles in which I travel.

11. Rely on discipline more than motivation.

12. Make the dream larger than the fear.

13. Speak in hushed tones; listen with intention.

14. Stay hope-filled, believe, have faith.

15. Be your own superhero.

16. Love myself as I love my loved ones.

These are the commitments I have made to myself.

Today, I failed.

Failed to meet my own expectations. Failed to have an answer when the struggle arrived. Failed to do what I believe I am capable of doing.

Today, I failed.

Here are lessons I took away from my failure:

1. Failure is not meant to be a dwelling: at best, it is a way station to where you are heading.

2. Failure is a recipe for success minus some important ingredients: the key is to figure out what is lacking.

3. Failure is not supposed to be easy to swallow: yet it must still be digested.

4. Failure is merely a time stamp: it can accurately measure only where you are right now.

5. Failure is not supposed to be sweet: When did medicine ever taste good?

6. Failure makes a statement about an attempt: it does not speak about who you are.

7. Failure is a whisper from the universe: "You are not there yet."

8. Failure actually is an option: but you have to set your bar really high to achieve it.

9. Failure is a dry-erase marker, not a permanent marker: it lasts long enough for the lesson to be learned, then it gets removed.

Today, I failed.

So tomorrow, I can be better.

Today, I failed. Again.

1. I failed to quit: I continued despite the growing struggle.

2. I failed to allow fear to win: I stared it down and it blinked.

3. I failed to just show up: I have dreams that demand more of me than simply making an appearance.

4. I failed to keep up with the Joneses: I am not in competition with them or anyone else.

5. I failed to settle on less than: I am deserving of so much more.

6. I failed to generate any excuses: I am too busy creating results.

7. I failed to lower my expectations for myself: I am permitted to have dreams currently beyond my ability to attain.

8. I failed to let the words of others be a part of my narrative: I alone am the author of the story being written.

9. I failed to let the failures of yesterday remain a part of my story: I erased them from the whiteboard.

Today, I failed.

Tomorrow, I am going to try to fail again.

I have known struggles, moments of hopelessness, burdens seemingly unbearable, and days of darkness. During those times, I have been left to answer, for myself, life's constant question: "Who are you to become?"

The only path away from the darkness that I knew was to work to become the me I wanted to be. And the closer I get to who I am to become, the less I struggle. When life asks me, "Who are you to become?"

I whisper, "I am to become . . .

More gentle
Less judgmental
More forgiving
Less bitter

More present
Less distracted
More light
Less shadow

More courageous
Less fear-filled
More daring
Less unwilling

More complete
Less fragmented
More giving
Less selfish

More alive
Less paralyzed
More loving
Less conditional"

I am to become, more or less, who I want to be. And that has saved me.

When things don't go as planned
Let go of expectations
Make an adjustment
Remember plan B
When little things hurt
Apply a bandage
Grow bigger
Remove the thorn
When the world is too loud
Turn down the volume
Quit listening to everyone else
Find time for the quiet
When you are feeling overwhelmed
Prioritize your priorities
Return to your center
Be okay with taking a break
When it just isn't working
Fix it
Renovate it
Replace it

When darkness arrives
Recall the sunlight
Light a candle
Become the torch
When stuff gets difficult
Ask for help
Step up your game
Simplify
When you're headed in the wrong direction
Turn around
Pump the brakes
Invest in a map
When you just don't want to
Choose discipline
Summon your strength
Just don't
When you realize you have choices
Excuses disappear
Problems get solved
You will know the power you have in your life.

I am not how long it takes me to finish
I am the effort I give in order to finish

I am not my number of victories or defeats
I am the times I found the courage to enter the fray

I am not concerned with the miles behind me
I am focused on finding the strength to go one more

I am not listening to the voices of "cannot"
I am silencing all but "I can"

I am not afraid of falling short anymore
I am more afraid of not spreading my wings

I am not merely the steps I am taking
I am also the moments I simply stood my ground

I am not the distance I have covered
I am all I have discovered along the way

I am not bound by expectations of others
I am free to live up to my own

I am not the impression others have of me
I am depths unseen, depths unexplored

What I am not has shown me all that I am.

Insatiably hungry
Rarely satisfied
Yet always content

Decidedly bent
Slightly broken
Yet in repair

Bone wearied
Muscle fatigued
Yet awakened

Ever wandering
Seemingly lost
Yet heading home

Restlessness
Breathlessness
Yet stillness

Sometimes doubting
Sometimes questioning
Yet somehow believing

Fighting battles
At war with demons
Yet at peace

Scars earned
Bruises, cuts, aches accepted
Yet comfortable in this skin

Forged in the flame
Dancing in the fire
Yet oh, the goose bumps

This is to dream
This is to live
Yet this is to be me.

Sometimes you just need to wing it.
Scrap the list
Lose the script
Ditch the plan

Sometimes you just need to wing it.
Get off the grid
Turn off notifications
Close the calendar

Sometimes you just need to wing it.
Don't ask for directions
Choose an unfamiliar path
Go where your heart leads

Sometimes you just need to wing it.
Stop crunching the numbers
Quit doing the math
Do it even if it doesn't add up

Sometimes you just need to wing it.
Break your own rules
Say, "To heck with conventional wisdom"
Refuse to conform

Sometimes you just need to wing it.
Surrender control
Let go of expectations
Just see what happens

Sometimes you just need to wing it.
Forget the recipe
Mix it up
Surprise yourself

Sometimes you just need to wing it.
Or you may never learn to fly.

I may not have strength to shed my burdens
But again today, I will work to become stronger

I may not understand the whys before me
But again today, I will remain faithful

I may not always get it right
But again today, I will show myself some grace

I may not have the courage to best my fears
But again today, I will bravely face them

I may not know where the path is leading me
But again today, I will trust the steps I'm taking

I may not see light at the end of the tunnel
But again today, I will stay on track

I may not be who I hope to become
But again today, I will strive to be all I am meant to be

I may not be completely healed
But again today, I will tend to the wounds

I may not achieve the dream I am dreaming
But again today, I will wake to continue the chase

Again today, I will.

The other side of me.

I walked out of the darkness that slowly settled deep within my crevices

I walked out of the fire that consumed the air I desperately needed to breathe

I walked out of the hopelessness that arrived without warning, seemingly without end

I walked out of a place of comfort that began to entomb me

I walked out of the fear that kept me clinging to the illusion of what was never real

I walked out of the noise that attempted to drown out the whispers of my heart

I walked out of the shattering that left the beautiful parts of me in pieces on the ground

I walked out to the other side of me.

A simple plan: keep on running.

Keep on running
Toward the light
Toward the dream
Toward the wild horizon

Keep on running
You may catch the wind
You may catch the unicorn
You may catch the impossible

Keep on running
The broken road
The uncharted path
The route your heart knows

Keep on running
Despite the ache
Despite the weariness
Despite the breathlessness

Keep on running
Something is out there
Something needs you to arrive
Something in the distance awaits

Keep on running
The miles offer a respite
The miles provide strength
The miles shape the warrior

Keep on running
It is to dance
It is to know flight
It is to set your life's pace

Keep on running, my friend.

Seven words to never forget: In time, it will all be okay.

Wounds heal, hearts mend, pain lessens, time soothes, memories remain, life continues. In the now, it may not feel like it, but you will be okay. This is life's promise.

Six words to never forget: Within you are all your answers.

You know what you want, you know how to achieve it, you know which road to take, you know where it will lead, you know when it is time. Inside, you know.

Five words to never forget: You are worthy of love.

As you are. You need not prove it. You need not change a single thing about you. You need not doubt it. You need not settle for less. And you need not be perfect. You need only to know your worth.

Four words to never forget: You can do this.

Whatever your "this" is, you can handle it. Your singular, most undeniable truth is that you are still standing. Despite it all, you made it here again today. And once more, you will find a way to get "this" done. Believe your truth.

Three words to never forget: Hope changes everything.

A hope-filled vessel will not sink. A hope-filled warrior will not be defeated. A hope-filled mind will not give over to fear. A hope-filled life will not be a life wasted. Be hope-filled.

Two words to never forget: Love endures.

All the love you have ever known is welled up inside you. It does not evaporate. It simply sits waiting for you to feel it and to use it as your source of fuel. Yes, loved ones pass. Loves of yesterday go on. But they left something within you: a reservoir of love. Swim in it.

One word to never forget: Breathe.

Breathe slowly. In time, it will all be okay. Breathe deeply. Within you are all your answers. Breathe in knowing. You are worthy of love. Breathe during the difficult moments. You can do this. Breathe in hope. Hope changes everything. Breathe out love. Love endures. Breathe. Just breathe.

I am not looking to take your place
I am wanting only to join you at the table
There is room here for all

I am not looking to steal your thunder
I am wanting only to come in from the storm
This must be a safe harbor

I am not looking to erase your story
I am wanting only to quietly pen my own
Each journey is worth reading

I am not looking to be the king
I am wanting only to be invited to the dance
This is to level the field

I am not looking to be better than you
I am wanting only to improve myself
And then we may all celebrate

I am not looking for anything unreasonable
I am wanting only to know how equity feels
Until then, I shall keep searching.

I see the fear well up in you
And I have faith you will find the courage to make it retreat

I see the hills rising before you
And I have faith you will find a way beyond them

I see the storm that has raged on around you
And I have faith you will seek higher ground

I see the burden being placed upon you
And I have faith you will find the strength not to buckle beneath it

I see the dream so far beyond your reach
And I have faith you will move forward until you grasp it

I see the struggle that has taken hold of you
And I have faith you will set yourself free

I see the heartache sent your way
And I have faith you will remember a broken heart still beats

I hope you see
I have faith in you.

Come, take hold of my trembling hand
And you will know of the fears that shake me

Come, carry my burden for a short while
And you will know why my pace has slowed

Come, sit in my gathering darkness
And you will know reasons the night offers me no rest

Come, feel me completely collapse
And you will know the strength it takes for me to rise

Come, hear the hopes I tightly cling to
And you will know the prayers I silently whisper

Come, listen to the broken rhythm of my heart
And you will know the pain beating within me

Come, know me
And you will never approach me without kindness, light, love, and grace.

Doing the math.

Many will watch in hopes that you fall
A few will watch in hopes that you rise

Many will stand in silent judgment of you
A few will stand in silent awe of you

Many will be placed in your way to slow you
A few will be placed in your way to guide you

Many will look on thinking you cannot do this
A few will look on believing you can

Many will criticize your decisions
A few will honor your decisions

Many will cheer only your missteps
A few will cheer your every step forward

Many will try to cast shadows upon your light
A few will try to bring light to your darkness

Many will celebrate being ahead of you
A few will celebrate you where you are

Many will never equal the impact of a few
A few will always outweigh the many

Do the math. A few > many.

If you want to be stronger, you must choose to operate from a place of strength.

Address your weaknesses. Have the critical conversations. Stand up for your goals. Stop berating and discounting yourself. Face your fears. Believe in yourself. This is strength.

If you want to be healthier, you must choose the "little more" option.

Move a little more. Smile a little more. Rest a little more. Give a little more. Hydrate a little more. Stretch a little more. Recover a little more. This is health.

If you want to grow, you must choose to move beyond what is comfortable.

Let go of excuses that keep you stuck. Do something you have never done. Quit quitting. Make new mistakes. Leap at a chance. Put your wings to the test. This is growth.

If you want to heal, you must choose to cleanse the wound.

Begin with forgiveness. Do not allow your past to infect your future. Stop re-reading the same chapter. Sit with the pain, but do not let it paralyze you. Be patient with yourself. Give yourself permission to mend. This is healing.

If you want love, you must choose to live with a heart wide open.

Give from your heart. See with your heart. Be gentle with the heart of another. Listen with your heart. Trust your heart's whispers. Never rein in your heart. Let your heart feel everything. This is love.

If you want to be a better version of you, you must choose. Strength. Health. Growth. Healing. Love.

Should I fall
I made a promise to myself
I will get back up

Should I question if I can
I made a promise to myself
I will believe in my abilities

Should strength be needed
I made a promise to myself
I will be strong enough

Should the struggle arrive
I made a promise to myself
I will keep moving through it

Should times become difficult
I made a promise to myself
I will be bigger than the moment

Should quitting be an option
I made a promise to myself
I will pick anything else

Should motivation not be enough
I made a promise to myself
I will stay disciplined

Should everything come undone
I made a promise to myself
I will keep my promises.

What has the upper hand in your life?
Faith or fear?

What do you give power to?
Trust or worry?

What consumes your time?
Blessings or stressings?

What thoughts do you pay attention to?
Positive or negative?

What belief do you hold closer?
"I can" or "I cannot"?

What lens do you filter your life through?
One of light or one of shadows?

What taste lingers from your past?
Sweetness or bitterness?

The what in your life determines the how in your life. How you respond. How you feel. How you face the day. How you see your life.

The how in your life then determines who you become in your life. For it is your responses, feelings, perceptions, and vision that ultimately define you.

In essence, there is a formula for becoming.

What + how = who

Pay attention to your what.

Manage your how.

Become who you are meant to be.

If you do not meet a goal
You are allowed to try again

If you take a few days away
You are allowed to pick up where you left off

If things do not go as planned
You are allowed to make a new plan

If you get a little off track
You are allowed to jump right back on

If you are tired of the drama
You are allowed to remove yourself from it

If you make a complete mess of things
You are allowed to forgive yourself

If you do not feel ready to leap
You are allowed to stop and catch your breath

If you are bowing beneath the burden
You are allowed to take a knee to gather strength

If you are weary from the noise
You are allowed to find your quiet

If you are needing some help
You are allowed to ask without shame

You are allowed to
If you simply allow yourself to.

To become more:

10. Believe more than you doubt.

9. Strive for more than comfort.

8. Talk to yourself more than you listen to yourself.

7. Trust more than you worry.

6. Look ahead more than you look behind.

5. Give more than you take.

4. Hustle for it more than you hope for it.

3. Dream of it more than you fear it.

2. Follow your heart more than you follow the crowd.

1. Love, more than anything.

To become more than, you must do more than.

If I let you in, I trust you.

I trust you with the fragile pieces of me
Please handle them with care
I trust you to sit unafraid of my darkness
Please do not fear when shadows arrive
I trust you to be there when hard times come
Please know I am not always strong enough

If I let you in, I believe in you.

I believe in you to tell me hard truths
Please don't shy away from an honesty I need
I believe in you to inspire me beyond this place
Please allow me to take hold of your cape
I believe in you to express patience with me
Please wait for me; I will arrive

If I let you in, I need you.

I need you to share the lessons you've learned
Please teach me how you survived the fall
I need you to shine your light upon my tears
Please show me; I too still glisten
I need you to believe in me
Please, when my own belief rebels, quell it

If I let you in, I love you.

I love you where words no longer exist
Please dance with me in this silent place
I love you as a part of me
Please understand that you now reside in me
I love you enough to let you in
Please close the door behind you.

I am not comfortable
There is a discomfort within me
Hard edges
Dark places
Jagged pieces

I am not comfortable
There is a discomfort about me
A restlessness
A relentlessness
A breathlessness

I am not comfortable
There is a discomfort to me
Born to dream
Born to wander
Born to struggle

I am not comfortable
There is a discomfort within me
Wounds not yet healed
Fears not yet overcome
Layers not yet discovered

I am not comfortable
There is a discomfort about me
Disinterested in the petty
Disconnected from the crowd
Discontented with the status quo

I am not comfortable
There is a discomfort to me
Been misled
Taken missteps
Oft misunderstood

I am not comfortable
There is a discomfort within me
If this makes you uncomfortable
I am comfortable with that.

Dear Friend,

If you come to me
with broken wings
I will walk with you
until you can fly once more

If you come to me
on bended knee
I will pray with you
until your strength returns

If you come to me
filled with darkness
I will sit with you
until the dawn breaks within you

If you come to me
afraid and trembling
I will hold you close
until the fear subsides

If you come to me
needing the silence
I will wait with you
in the quiet breathlessness

If you come to me
in search of refuge
I will invite you
into my heart

If you come to me
I will be here for you.

Love,

Me

Tips for having your very best race:

1. Head up: You belong. With this simple knowing, anything becomes possible.

2. Eyes forward: What is behind you is there for a reason. Leave it there.

3. Be present: Fully absorb the moment. In the now, nothing can grow so large that you cannot handle it.

4. Feel everything: Deny nothing. Let everything in. It all serves a purpose. Fear, goose bumps, doubt, joy. It is all part of the story.

5. Chase no one: Much is lost for trying to hold another's pace. Seek your own. If chase you must, let it be of things wild and untamed. Of things you can never hold.

6. Loosely hold the reins: Do not grip so tightly that tension locks you up, but keep ahold. Nothing is gained for being completely out of control.

7. Be mindful of others: Your dreams and hopes matter, yet no more than those of another. You are important and special, yet no more so than another. Do nothing to impede another's progress.

8. Defy gravity: At its worst, it is a constant stumble forward. At its best, it provides precious moments of flight. In either case, the key is to remain upright.

9. Earn your finish: In a world where almost everything can be bought or sold, discounted or imitated, maintain your integrity. Do all the work. Own your best and worst results.

10. Leave nothing untapped: You begin with little more than a heartbeat and hopes. Move in such a way as others come to know your heart. Move in such a way as to inspire hope in others. Empty yourself.

Tips for having your very best life.

These are some race day essentials.

Acceptance: News flash! Things are going to happen. Things outside of your control. Things that make it more difficult. Accept them. Have the presence and resolve to find a way beyond them. Do not allow the problem to be where you stop. Be solution-oriented, not problem-focused. Accept, adjust, succeed. A plan far more effective than complain, remain stuck, offer excuses.

Patience: Do not get caught up in the frenzy and flurry of movement of others. You know your rhythm. Keep to it. Do not forget to forgive others. In their hurry, they will make mistakes that may impact you. You are not above this humanness. Breathe through it. Do not escalate out of your own nervousness. There is a quiet place within you. Settle into it.

Fuel: Get good sustenance for your thoughts so you do not begin feeding off the negative. It is an easy reach. So often you begin to consume fuel that is not a good source of energy—fear, doubt, past failures, old excuses. You gobble those up. Instead, you need to pick those things that will sustain you because they completely fill your tank. "I can." "I will." "I am capable." "I am strong." Reach for those.

Unwavering belief: Keep your faith. There are things you believe at your very core. Things that you never waver upon. Things larger than yourself. Hold onto those in the most trying and difficult moments, whatever they are for you. A higher power. The power of prayer. Nothing is impossible. Everything is possible. Your capacity to endure. Magic. Hope.

Gratitude: What if everything that ever happens or happened to you is simply an opportunity for you to say thank you? Would that change how you view challenges, obstacles, and hardships? Would that change your response to difficult people, difficult moments, and difficult situations? In these moments before you, express thanks. It may change everything. Try it.

Perspective: Above all, keep your lens wide open. Nothing that happens today, good or bad, defines you. You are not an event, a number, a time, a goal, an outcome. When your focal point becomes so narrowed, you lose sight of all the things that ultimately define you. Those things brought you to this place. And they will remain intact, long after this passes. Maintain your perspective.

Those are some everyday essentials.

A new twist on an old take.

"I am in competition only with myself."

Trust me, I get it. It is all about being better than you once were. Self-improvement and not comparing yourself to another. I get it. I just decided that it is in my better interest to stop competing with myself.

Too often, it has been more a fight against myself for not liking who I am. For feeling I was or am not good enough.

Too often, it has gone from beating yesterday to beating myself up for not being farther along my path. For feeling I was lacking or deficient.

I just decided that it is in my better interest to start cooperating with myself.

So if you see me talking to myself, know that my words will be less harsh, less judgmental, less critical.

So if you see me taking a break, know that I am at peace where I am, enjoying the rest, catching my breath.

So if you see me smiling after I fall short, know that I am proud of my effort, grateful for the chance, realizing this isn't the end.

So if you see me and I cannot tell you how far I've come or how far I've yet to go, know that I am enjoying being here, not measured by distance, where I need and want to be.

So if you see me appearing less worried, know that I am trusting myself more, building faith in myself, learning to believe.

So if you see me tending to my wounds, know that I am not broken, I am healing, I am going to be okay.

So if you see me looking at myself, know that I love the reflection I see, I can see my beauty, I now view myself through my own lens.

So if you see me treating myself with dignity, compassion, and love, know that I am worthy of everything I offer others.

So if you see me being completely me, know that I am in cooperation with myself.

Things to remember:

1. There are times you must consciously remember to breathe.

2. Remember how important "please" and "thank you" are.

3. Take a moment to remember what you are truly wanting for yourself.

4. Not everyone will see things your way; remember, that is okay.

5. You only have so much energy; remember to prioritize how you spend it.

6. Remember when you decided to stand up for yourself? Do it again.

7. If you remember your why, what you must do becomes apparent.

8. Wherever you are, remember to be there.

9. People will attempt to rain on your parade; remember, you are waterproof.

10. Others will believe what they believe about you; remember, what they believe does not make it your truth.

11. Remember, the path of your regret has been paved mostly by your excuses.

12. It's simple. Remember your strength.

13. When darkness arrives, remember, no matter how deep, it cannot envelope light.

14. Remember, a heart continues to beat, even when broken.

15. Remember, you are primarily defined by the words you speak after "I am . . ."

16. Remember, somebody loves and needs you.

17. You are beautiful. Remember to view yourself only through that lens.

How to win your next race, in five steps:

1. Show up: Do you even realize what a victory it is to get up, show up, and go about the business of living a good, hard life? That is most of the battle. Keep showing up. Just keep showing up.

2. Outdistance your excuses: Get ahead of what keeps you from getting ahead. I know, I know. You cling to your excuses because they keep you from getting hurt. They keep you from failing. Guess what? Those are just more excuses. Move on.

3. Watch your watch: Stop looking at everyone else's. True story: I'm not racing against you. I've never stolen your finish line. Nor do I want to. Nor can I. That belongs only to you. Sure, be inspired by others, but do not discount what you achieve. When you get to your finish line, I will cheer for you. When I get to mine, I hope you will do the same.

4. Climb on: Do not fear the hills. Lean into them. This is where your strength is found. With strength comes belief. Where there is belief, the calm comes. Amid the calm, you will realize you are bigger than your hills. And soon you are beyond them.

5. Own your finish: Stop explaining your results. Let them stand on their own, and accept them. You do an injustice when "would have" and "could have" become part of your story. Truth is, the result is what you accomplished. End of story. Find a way to celebrate that you showed up, bested your excuses, focused on yourself, and got past your hills. That defines winning.

How to win at your life, in five steps.

Third Law of Motion: for every action, there is an equal and opposite reaction.

I was wrong
I said, "I am sorry"
I was offered a chance
I took it

I had nothing to say
I simply listened
I had my excuses
I decided not to use them

I felt myself slipping
I held onto hope
I fell to my knees
I offered my silent prayer

I was feeling stressed
I took time to breathe
I was unsure of which way to go
I decided to follow my heart

I could not scale my Everest
I found another way beyond it
I could not hear my heartbeat
I learned to quiet the noise

I was confronted with hate
I showed them love
I knew heartbreak
I stitched myself back together

I knew love
I gave it all my heart

Most Important Law of Motion: your reaction determines whether you move backward or forward.

How to run a marathon.

With respect
With patience
Without fear
Without blinders

Properly rested
Properly fueled
Fueled by faith
Fueled by strength

Undaunted
Untethered
One stride at a time
One breath at a time

Not looking behind you
Not looking too far ahead
Keep your head up
Keep your hopes up

Steady your pace
Steady your nerves
Fully aware it is difficult
Fully aware it is possible

By following the signs
By following your heart
Believing in miracles
Believing in yourself

Begin from a place of gratitude
Begin from a place of love
Along the way, find opportunities to offer a smile, a thanks, a high five
Along the way, find your joy

Finish with no regret
Finish with nothing more to give

How to live your life.

Thoughts about training:

1. Training is extremely personal. There is "no one size fits all." Do not force the fit.

2. If rest is not part of the plan, something is wrong with the plan.

3. Pushing your limit is perfectly fine, but know when to limit your pushing.

4. It is not that you do not trust the training; it is that you do not trust yourself. Knock that off.

5. A goal of any training is improvement. Do not be afraid to measure your growth. Test yourself. Sign up for the competition. Enter the race. Do that thing.

6. Training yourself to be disciplined enough to do the training is a key to successful training.

7. Training increases your capacity to physically endure. However, you must mentally embrace this principle.

8. Training smarter trumps merely training harder. Training is a process of learning. Educate yourself.

9. Training implies an active, ongoing process; therefore, you do not arrive all at once. You gradually get there. Be patient.

10. If you have done the training, the results will reflect it.

Thoughts about living.

I will not be afraid, for I already know how the race will go. I need simply to run it.

I will begin
I will feel strong
I will grow wings
I will know flight

I will catch my breath
I will keep moving
I will open my heart
I will feel love

I will smile
I will struggle
I will continue
I will climb

I will falter
I will know heartbreak
I will move beyond it
I will grow weary

I will not give up
I will experience joy
I will turn toward home
I will finish

I will have given it all away
I will be celebrated

I will not be afraid, for I already how the story will go. I need simply to live it.

It really is quite simple.

If you are thankful
Express it

If you can give back
Do it

If you have been blessed
Pay it forward

If you know joy
Share it

If a light is shone upon you
Reflect it

If you are grateful
Show it

If you know what is most important
Act on it

If you have an abundance
Give it away

If you have been loved
Be about it

If you want a beautiful life
Keep it simple.

It's just about time.

Time to turn down the volume: Quiet the noise, little one. Listen not to the echoes of those who do not believe. Listen not to the doubts that call from the darkness. Turn down the volume. And in the quiet, only your breath and heartbeat will be heard. One speaks to your calm. One speaks to your strength. This is all you ever need to listen to.

Time to turn inward: Stop looking at what others are doing. This is a distraction, as is anything that takes away from your journey. Conserve your energy. Know your energy drains and remove yourself from them. Establish your priorities. Do not waver from them. Be about what you need. This is not selfishness. This is taking care of yourself.

Time to heal: You must rest, little one. Your body is now tired. Your mind is now weary. Both must be healed, cared for. Slow your harried pace. Slow your frenzied thoughts. It will all come together, for the work has been done. What remains is simply the time between now and what you will surely accomplish. A rested body will reward you. A rested mind will propel you. This is what healing looks like.

Time to spring-clean: Consider all the baggage you are still holding onto. To what purpose? It merely takes up space, weighs you down, keeps you from moving forward. Fears, regrets, past failures, worn excuses. The baggage. Get rid of it. Now is all about renewal, cleansing, removing the clutter. Unencumbered, the hills will not seem so difficult, the finish not so far, the dream not so impossible. This is to run free.

It's about time.

Ways to become unstressed.

Unlock: Unlock yourself from yesterday. You need not remain a prisoner to it. It is called the past because you are past it. It is stationary. You have moved beyond it. It is unable to be changed. You are changing. Let it go.

Untangle: Untangle yourself from doubt. You are so wrapped up in it that it has become a straitjacket. It is difficult to achieve anything bound by doubt. If you simply believed as hard as you doubted, you would free yourself.

Unfollow: Unfollow the pace, path, and drama of others. So much of your stress is the result of paying too much attention to what others are doing. Whether you are trying to keep up with them, attempting to walk their way, or playing into their drama, it is energy and time wasted. Go your own way.

Unattach: Unattach yourself from the opinion of others. Absolutely nothing anyone thinks about you or says about you alters your truth. And yet, if a single negative opinion is uttered, you let it attach itself to you like cling wrap. Firmly grasp your own undeniable truth about yourself. Everything else is just noise.

Unpopulate: Unpopulate your "friends" list. You do not require 2,718 friends. You need six. One to tell you hard, real truths. One to whisper, "Hello, beautiful." One to fan your flame. One to sit with your darkness. One with whom to dance. One who will always be there.

Unearth: Unearth your inner child. So long ago, you hid away that magical, beautiful, loving being. Giggle. Smile. Sing. Dance. Hug. Share. Imagine. Create. Dream. Dare. Take naps. Make believe. Do all things with joy. Return to that child.

Unstress yourself.

Things you need never fear:

1. The starting line: If you must fear, be afraid to never start. Be afraid to never fail. You need never fear beginnings. They offer possibilities, opportunities, and awakenings. Seek out as many starting lines as you can. As you stand before them, you will begin to get a sense of who you can become.

2. The distant hills: Looming in the distance, they appear as mountains, as if they are insurmountable. You need never fear the climb. You see, the hills ahead are simply waiting for you to be strong enough to conquer them. And if you keep moving toward them, you are gaining that strength.

3. The rolling thunder: Do not seek shelter. Do not cower. You need never fear the thunder. It is simply the clap of the universe, signaling that the storm has arrived. You are the storm. And the universe offers its applause.

4. The dream given to you: The dream has not been placed within you for safekeeping. You need never fear showing off your dream. It is not intended to be buried and locked away. Take it out. Try it on for size. If it does not fit, do not shrink it. Rather, grow into it.

5. The finishing time: You need never fear the numbers displayed. For your greatest triumph will occur when you embrace this singular truth: There is no calculating device capable of measuring your worth. It simply reflects that you found the courage to start, had the strength to climb, became the storm, and grew into the dream. And that is a victory.

You need never fear.

Imagine.

I am looking forward to the goose bumps. The emerging butterflies. The not knowing. The wondering.

I am looking forward to the beginning. The anticipation. The new opportunity. The first step.

I am looking forward to the coming together. The preparation. The plan. The physical and mental merging.

I am looking forward to the stillness. The place where calm takes over. The place where fear does not reside. The place where the noise fades.

I am looking forward to the dream unfolding. The reality of it all. The impossible no longer true. The wild horizon drawing near.

I am looking forward to the ups and downs. The change of pace both bring. The challenge both present. The patience each demands.

I am looking forward to the unraveling. The growth amid the suffering. The discovery of a way through. The forging of a warrior.

I am looking forward to the celebration. The kiss upon my lips. The overcoming heartbreak. The turning for home.

Imagine. How amazing would this life be if you simply lived it, looking forward?

If you had only one week left . . .

Would you spend it filling yourself with worry or live it filled with wonder?

Would you spend it complaining about things you cannot control or live it so completely that there was no time for complaints?

Would you spend it angered by little things that do not go right or live it seeking joy in all the little things?

Would you spend it shouting your grievances or live it speaking your gratitudes?

Would you spend it collecting your fears or live it gathering your faith?

Would you spend it regretting what you had not done or live it rejoicing in all you accomplished?

Would you spend it making excuses or live it making memories?

Would you spend it cursing the outcome or live it celebrating the journey?

Would you spend it believing it was the worst week of your life or live it believing you were blessed with one more week?

If you had only one week left.

I hope you live it.

Essentials for the storm:

1. Knowing: Know this—you are waterproof. Know this—you are going to get wet, and it does not mean you are drowning. Know this—you've always known how to swim.

2. Realization: Realize you cannot control the weather, only how you prepare for it. Realize faith is shelter from the storm. Realize the storm ends; it is not the end.

3. Endurance: Endure, for every storm passes. Every single one. Endure, for the storm eventually produces the rainbows. Endure, for the strongest of all things weather the storm.

4. Hope: Hope floats. Hope is a life preserver. Hope allows the sun to shine despite the gathering clouds.

5. Resilience: Resilience, for power can always be restored. Resilience, for broken fences can always be mended. Resilience, for the dream can always be resurrected.

Essentials for the storm. Don't leave home without them.

part two: truths

living with authenticity

If you tell the truth, you don't have to remember anything.
—Mark Twain

Seven truths about running a marathon:

1. If you are willing to begin, somewhere within you is the will to finish.

2. Being afraid—well, that happens. Being brave—well, that is a decision.

3. At some point in time, you will be challenged. Knowing that, you should already know what your response will be.

4. You can stress about the impending weather. Or you can create a climate within you that is impervious to it.

5. Relinquish the need to compare your pace to that of another. You share the same course, but no one is running the same race.

6. If you are not celebrating the journey, you may have lost sight of the goal.

7. The single greatest fuel you can carry is the belief you hold about your capacity to endure.

Seven truths about running your life.

Truths I know about you:

1. You are more than fragile: Yes, I understand, pieces of you have been made to break. Hearts are made that way. They were never designed to harden. Bones are made that way. They were never designed to handle every stress. And so both can be shattered. And yet a broken heart still beats. A broken bone becomes stronger. You were designed with the power to heal. Do not live fearing the brokenness. You are more than fragile.

2. You are capable of learning: Mistakes get made. Failing happens. Welcome to your own humanness. You are flawed. That is a complete statement. It is all a part of your wiring. But your greatness does not exist in your perfection. It is born from your capacity to learn from your mistakes and failings. This is what leads to your growth. This is what brings about change within you. This is what propels you forward. You are capable of learning.

3. You are becoming: Perhaps this is a significant source of frustration for you. You want to already *be*. Better. Stronger. Farther. Healed. Complete. Life does not operate that way. Life is the art of continuously unfolding. And there is a beauty and magic to this art. For no matter where you are in the process of unfolding, you are exactly where you are supposed to be. How amazing is that? So do not rush. You are becoming.

4. You are going to be all right: That is how every single chapter in your book has always ended. Always. I know it doesn't always feel that way. And yet, when a new chapter begins, it is because you made it through. And every single time, it was the result of you facing a fear, finding a way to rise to your feet, besting a demon, or letting go of what had to go. You will do again what needs to be done. You are going to be all right.

Truths I know about you. Because you are living proof.

All of this.

Hills. More hills.
Speed. More speed.
Treadmill miles. Assault bike calories.
Rower meters. Ski erg pulls.

Early morning alarms. Late night workouts.
Weekend miles. Weekday weights.
CrossFit. Cross my heart.
Crossing days off. Crossing finish lines.

Blisters. Bruises.
Little pains. Nagging aches.
Burpees. Lunges.
Squats. Sled drags.

Sit-ups. Pull-ups.
Push-ups. Just get up.
Sweat. Soreness.
Tired. Grinding.

Heart. Tenacity.
Fight. Grit.
Rest days. Hump days.
Snow days. Run days.

One more rep. One more mile.
One more try. One more fail.
Easy miles. Long miles.
Taper miles. All the miles.

Days I didn't want to. Days I couldn't wait to.
Days I didn't think I could. Days I knew I would.

All of that.

So I never have to answer the question "Why did you quit?"

If it is love, it does not boast of what it offers
It quietly and simply gives

If it is love, it does not ever lose faith
It continues to believe

If it is love, it does not seek the spotlight
It looks to reflect the light

If it is love, it does not fear a difficult path
It is willing to walk wherever the road leads

If it is love, it does not accept credit
It keeps no score, holds no debt

If it is love, it does not leave during the storm
It is the safest of havens

If it is love, it does not quell the dream
It is the torch that sets things ablaze

If it is love, it does not seek to rescue
It will provide all the DIY tools

If it is love, it does not know its truth worth
It is immeasurable.

This is love.

Dear Friend,

Rest easy this night.

Find comfort in knowing this one simple, immutable truth: you created this opportunity.

It was not born of luck or happenstance. It was not made merely of wishes, hopes, or daydreams.

Every time you decided to get back up, you created this opportunity.

Every time you chose discipline over excuse, you created this opportunity.

Every time you pushed yourself the extra mile, you created this opportunity.

Every time you ignored the doubts and fears, you created this opportunity.

Every time you overcame the urge to call it quits, you created this opportunity.

Every time you did not bow before the difficult, you created this opportunity.

Every time you refused to accept impossible as a truth, you created this opportunity.

Every time you found the courage to believe in yourself, you created this opportunity.

Every time you braved the raging storm, you created this opportunity.

Rest easy, my friend. You were created for this.

Love,

Me

Race reflections:

1. You begin with little more than hopes and fears. How you finish depends on which you choose as your fuel.

2. When you realize you cannot outrun your fear, you stop inviting it to the race.

3. It can be a competition or celebration. With one, you stand a good chance of not winning. With the other, you never stand a chance of losing. Choose to celebrate it.

4. Be ready for the storm, but always expect the sunshine.

5. Physical preparation brings you to the start. Mental preparation brings you home. Both are necessary.

6. Strength is required for the climb, but first, you must believe yourself capable of reaching the summit.

7. If you run carrying doubt, you will find signs that give you reason to further doubt. If you run carrying faith, you will find signs that give you reason to further believe.

8. Weakness finds a foothold only when you forget how strong you are.

9. If you dare to open yourself completely to the challenge, you will find the pieces buried within you made for one purpose: to overcome.

10. The greatest respect you can demonstrate is to offer no excuses.

11. Being grateful is not a singular act; it is a way of being.

12. You once did this for the sheer joy of it. If that now is your only reason, it is enough.

Life reflections.

Running is . . .

1. Equal parts flying and landing: you mustn't fear either phase

2. A search for stillness: to move without being hurried

3. A matter of the heart: where there is heartbreak, there is also love

4. Best done looking forward: looking behind you will eventually trip you up

5. Rarely about a number: the best of all things are rarely measurable

6. Natural, but still not easy: you were born for it, yet it brings its challenges

7. A test of endurance: no matter the length

8. Constantly varied: what it will bring is seldom known

9. Paradoxical: it leaves you empty while filling you up

10. For the courageous: it takes a special brand of bravery to keep showing up

11. Weathering in action: building you up, tearing you down, building you up . . . until you are made complete

12. The pursuit of memories: perhaps those alone are worth the chase

13. A gift: honor it, cherish it, celebrate it, love it

Life is . . .

When it comes to running a marathon, you must remember this: there are demons out there, simply waiting.

1. Yesterday: because yesterday knows almost everything about you. And it shows up to remind you. It whispers constantly in your ear. Yesterday you failed. Yesterday you came up short. Yesterday you quit. Yesterday you were not strong enough. Yesterday you said, "I can't." The more you listen, the more you begin to believe in yesterday. To defeat this demon, you must remember this: It does not know everything about you. It does not know who you are today.

2. Fear: what consumes so much of our fuel. It requires energy and oxygen to grow. And we so often breathe life into it. We feed it. And then we wonder why we are so paralyzed. It is simple. We now have no fuel of our own. Fear. Fear of not knowing. Fear of not finishing. Fear of not attaining some mythical number. To defeat this demon, you must remember this: What you constantly feed will surely grow. Put your energy into feeding your faith. Not only will your faith grow, it will also choke off the fear.

3. Pain: It will pay a visit. For some, it will be gradual and exquisite. For others, it will be immediate and excruciating. But it will arrive. No one is immune to it. Eventually everyone gets exposed to the blade. It can cut superficially. It can cut savagely deep. It can take on many forms. As a rawness. As a brokenness. As a hopelessness. To defeat this demon, you must remember this: Everything that ever cut you failed to stop you. You found a way to keep moving, you healed, and you will do so again this time.

4. Emptiness: What happens when you begin to fall off pace? What happens when you feel the dream slowly slipping away? What happens when the elements conspire to wear you down? It begins to creep up on you. This emptiness. This void. It starts to feel as if everything was for naught. And you begin to try to fill the emptiness with concessions, frustrations, excuses. But it only grows larger. To defeat this demon, you must remember this: Emptiness can be filled only from a place of abundance. Within you, you have strength, faith, and hope in great abundance. Call on them.

5. Loneliness: You can be surrounded by thousands and yet feel so all alone. For the race is yours alone to run. And it will seem as if no one knows exactly what you are going through. No one knows of your yesterday. No one knows of the fear you feel. No one knows of the pain that now consumes you. No one knows of the emptiness you carry with you. To defeat this demon, you must remember this: You never truly do this alone. While no one can know, someone is carrying you in their heart, thoughts, and prayers. And that someone is waiting for you to arrive.

When it comes to living this life, you must remember this: there are demons out there, simply waiting to be defeated.

Asking for a friend.

Did you show up?
That's amazing!
Many are too afraid to take on the challenge and thus they never show up.

Did you give it the best you had on that day?
That's amazing!
Many are too afraid to risk failing and thus they never push themselves.

Did you make the best decision for yourself?
That's amazing!
Many are too afraid of what others might think and thus they never do what's in their own best interest.

Did you fight for your finish?
That's amazing!
Many are too afraid of the battle and thus they never become the warrior.

Did you remember to celebrate yourself?
That's amazing!
Many are too afraid of cheering for themselves and thus they never hear the applause.

Did you remember?
You are amazing!

The path to happiness.

Quit worrying about what others think. When do you finally stop investing energy here?

Quit looking around to see who's watching. Your business is to mind your business. They are not your business. They are just up in your business. It isn't the same.

Quit listening for the voice of others. Your voice is the only one you need to hear. They do not speak for you. They speak about you. It isn't the same.

The path to happiness.

Quit worrying about getting somewhere. When do you finally get to enjoy where you are?

Quit wishing away this place where you now stand. Think about how hard you fought to get this far. That is a victory. Settle in for a moment to simply celebrate arriving right here.

Quit wishing away this very now. So much about you has become time-sensitive. Time is now a stressor. Additionally, you've forgotten the most important moment: right now. Much changes when you come to value the time at hand.

The path to happiness.

Quit worrying about being perfect. When does this stop becoming a goal?

Quit telling yourself that isn't the goal. You want the perfect picture. The perfect run. The perfect time. You stress over the smallest of details, hoping everything is perfect. And mostly because you worry about what others will think. Interesting.

Quit telling yourself there will be a perfect time. It keeps you in a holding pattern. By putting off doing that thing, you put your life on hold. If there is to be a perfect time, it is now. Take the trip. Chase the dream. Do that thing.

The path to happiness.

Quit worrying.

It is not that I am not interested in idle conversation.
I just care more about hearing of your loves, your heart's whispers, that which leaves you breathless.

It is not that I am not interested in the mundane.
I just care more about knowing of your silent dreams, your waking fears, that which commands your fullest attention.

It is not that I am not interested in the din of the crowd.
I just care more about feeling the comfortable silence, leaning into the whispered tones, that which is expressed when words are no longer adequate.

It is not that I am not interested in what you believe.
I just care more about seeing if actions belie or confirm beliefs, finding out if talk is merely talk, the truth that you are living.

It is not that I am not interested in the chains you wear.
I just care more about what sets you free, the pieces of you yearning to soar, that which takes you to a higher place.

It is not that I am not interested in what broke you.
I just care more about how you are stitching yourself back together, the texture and layers of your scars, that which causes you to still rise.

It is not that I am not interested.
I just care more.

I'm looking forward.

I'm looking forward. To the possibilities. To all that could or might be. To chances for growth. To challenges that will shape me. I'm looking forward to the dreams that still whisper my name.

I'm looking forward. With faith. For I have conquered my hills. Survived the heartbreak. Braved the storms. I'm moving forward with faith, for I found a way to keep moving despite the hills, heartbreak, and storms.

I'm looking forward. New paths to be wandered. Places I've never been. Adventures waiting to be taken. Wild horizons yet to be seen. I'm looking forward, new paths to be wandered for this ever-restless soul.

I'm looking forward. No turning back. Yesterday already lived. The distance already covered. The memories already locked away. I'm looking forward, no turning back; today is already waiting to be lived.

I'm looking forward. Mind wide open. My vow to learn. Arms open wide. My victory pose. Heart wide open. My permission to love. I'm looking forward, completely open wide, and finally free.

I'm looking forward.

I offer these hypotheses.

If it appears dark,
Then perhaps you need only to open your eyes

If it keeps coming undone,
Then perhaps you need to consider it broken

If it cannot be changed,
Then perhaps you need to give up trying to control it

If it will not heal,
Then perhaps you need to stop clawing at the wound

If it continues to frighten you,
Then perhaps you need to determine exactly what you are so afraid of

If it is a constant source of stress,
Then perhaps you need to remove it from your to-do list

If it does not contribute to your growth,
Then perhaps you need to simply let it go

If it is not speaking your truth,
Then perhaps you need to hit the mute button

If it keeps whispering to your heart,
Then perhaps you need to listen more closely

If it nourishes your soul,
Then perhaps you need to keep inviting it to the table

If it adds to your happiness,
Then perhaps you need more of it in your life

I offer these hypotheses.

Perhaps you need to test them out.

I ask myself: *What is it worth?*

Is it worth my serenity?

Shall I rise up in this moment, giving over to the rant or rage? Shall I fall victim to anger?

Or shall I rise above in this moment, giving over to acceptance and grace? Shall I stand calm against the storm?

Is it worth my happiness?

Shall I surrender my internal joy to an external force? Shall I allow this most prized possession to be stolen?

Or shall I surrender the idea that anything possesses such power? Shall I realize what I have chosen cannot be wrested from me?

Is it worth my heart?

Shall I go all in on the fleeting and the temporary? Shall I risk breaking for what is not able to hold me together?

Or shall I commit fully to that which is fully committed? Shall I give my love only to that which can bear all of me?

Is it worth my worth?

Shall I accept this discount, head down and bowed? Shall I hide my light, make myself small?

Or shall I discount the discount, choosing instead to value my own value? Shall I shine brightly, beautifully, boldly?

I ask myself: *What is it worth?*

For within the question, I come to know what it is I shall do.

Everything changes when you allow yourself . . .

To love who you are

To be yourself

To seek your own path

To not be bound by convention

To dance your own dance

To enjoy this life

To revel in the journey

To grant yourself permission

To chase the wild horizon

To not stress the little things

To be fearless

To have complete faith in yourself

To live and love passionately

To not be so worried about perceptions

To define yourself

To be joy-filled

To see yourself as beautiful

Everything changes when you allow yourself.

I decided to give up.

I decided to give up running
From the fears I hold
Toward a past I cannot catch

I decided to give up working out
My frustrations on others
The need to always be right

I decided to give up lifting
Others onto a pedestal
The white flag of surrender

I decided to give up flexing
My ego when I need help
My need to control everything

I decided to give up competing
With anyone who is not me
Against perfection

I decided to give up racing
Through this moment
When patience is required

I decided to give up stretching
My excuses into habits
One chapter into my entire story

I decided to give up trying to win
At the expense of others
Because life isn't a contest

I decided to give up.

Best decision I ever made.

When will you finally hear the words I speak to you?

"Hello, beautiful"

"You are amazing"

"Do not fear"

"I trust you"

"You can do this"

"I believe in you"

"You are worthy"

"Trust more; worry less"

"I am in awe of you"

"You are more than enough"

"I love you"

When will you finally hear the words I speak to you?

When they are finally the words you speak to yourself.

I would rather be talked to
Than be talked about

I would rather fail magnificently
Than fail to even try

I would rather follow my own heart
Than follow the path of the masses

I would rather my silence be misunderstood
Than my words not be heard

I would rather feel the deepest of wounds
Than feel nothing at all

I would rather a truth tear me completely apart
Than have a lie be what holds me together

I would rather seek the promised rainbow
Than seek shelter from the possible storm

I would rather be seen as a foolish dreamer
Than be foolish enough to never chase a dream

I would rather love like there's no tomorrow
Than wait until tomorrow to begin to love

I would rather live having not feared dying
Than die having feared living.

Keys to being a successful runner:

1. Guard against doubt: It is an infectious disease. Vaccinate yourself against it.

2. Fully commit: Go all in. Half-hearted, more often than not, leads to brokenhearted.

3. Endure failing: Failure is not an ending. It must simply be endured as part of your evolution.

4. Stretch: In all things, stay flexible. And reach for what you cannot currently touch.

5. Prepare for the difficult: You may not know when difficulties will arrive. But you can be prepared for them when they do.

6. Lean forward: It seems easy enough. But this requires that you trust you will not fall. Ironically, that becomes the tipping point.

7. Stop fearing the climb: If you are to rise above your current situation, you must be willing to climb. Seek out a mountain.

8. Move with grace: This way, you do less damage to yourself. Be forgiving, be kind, be gentle but fierce, be open to change.

9. Go slow to go fast: Build your runway first. Only then can you launch yourself.

10. Remain humble: Your victories will be seen. You need not magnify them.

Keys to being a successful human.

I will not be defined by my failures
I choose instead to be defined by how I respond to my failures

I will not be defined by my success
I choose instead to be defined by how I use my success to help others succeed

I will not be defined by what cut me
I choose instead to be defined by how I showed grace and forgiveness

I will not be defined by my scars
I choose instead to be defined by how I decided to heal

I will not be defined by any number
I choose instead to be defined by what cannot be counted

I will not be defined by what was taken from me
I choose instead to be defined by what I have left to give

I will not be defined by my heaviest fears
I choose instead to be defined by the ounce of courage that shows up to face them

I will not be defined by the weaknesses that often take me down
I choose instead to be defined by the strength it takes to rise once more

I will not be defined by the whispers of others
I choose instead to be defined by the quiet actions that speak to who I am

I will not be defined by the yesterday I lived
I choose instead to be defined by how I shall live today

I will not be defined
I choose instead to redefine who I ever thought I could become.

What you don't need and what you need to be a happier, healthier you.

You don't need equipment to exercise
You need discipline to exercise

You don't need to defeat anyone else
You need to defeat your own excuses

You don't need to beat the clock
You need to stop beating yourself up

You don't need to justify your decision
You need to just act upon your decision

You don't need be perfect
You need to be perfectly okay with being you

You don't need to follow the latest trend
You need to follow the course designed for you

You don't need a "what you have to do" list
You need a "how you want to be" list

You don't need to be a people pleaser
You need to make yourself happy

You don't need to have or be anything more
You need to have an understanding that you are enough

What you don't need and what you need to be a happier, healthier you.

Take what you need. Leave what you don't.

I'm not even close to perfect
And I'm okay with that
Because I'm sure it was never the goal

I'm not altogether put together
And I'm okay with that
Because I'm slowly gathering the pieces

I'm not quite sure where I'm going
And I'm okay with that
Because I'm still plotting the course

I'm not in control of all the outcomes
And I'm okay with that
Because I'm responsible only for the input

I'm not able to meet everyone's expectations
And I'm okay with that
Because I'm not interested in trying to

I'm not better, stronger, faster than others
And I'm okay with that
Because I'm not competing with anyone

I'm not who others may need me to be
And I'm okay with that
Because I'm exactly who I want to be

I'm not beautiful in everyone's eyes
And I'm okay with that
Because I'm able to see me without their filter

I'm not always okay
And I'm okay with that
Because I'm aware that I will be.

My Friend,

Before you rest this night, I need you to know a few things.

I need you to know just how strong you are. Nothing in this day was able to defeat you. You are still standing. Remember this.

I need you to know just how courageous you are. You faced all the things this day brought to you. You are now on the other side of them. Remember this.

I need you to know just how amazing you are. You showed up again this day. Your streak remains intact and unbroken. Remember this.

I need you to know just how powerful you are. You made the most powerful choice one can make this day: to live your life. Remember this.

I need you to know just how much I need you. I looked to you, again this day, to show me how to be brave and strong. And once again, you did. Remember this.

I need you to know just how loved you are. You are held gently in the hearts of many. And they want you to know they love you. Remember this.

Before you rest this night, I need you to remember a few things.

Love,

Me

Dear Mom,

You have always been my rock. And yet you were always the softest place to land.

You have always been my anchor. And yet you were always the one to breathe wind into my sails.

You have always been my guide. And yet you were always following along behind me.

You have always been my greatest source of light. And yet you were always unaware of your own brilliance.

You have always been my support system. And yet you were always teaching me how to stand on my own.

You have always been my greatest fan. And yet you were always the one I looked up to.

You have always been my hero. And yet you were always the one who made me believe I was super.

You have always been there. And yet, should I have to one day face this world without you, you will still always be.

I love you, Mom.

Your grateful and loving child.

If you want anything, you must commit fully to that thing.

If you want happiness, you must choose to lead a joy-filled existence. This must be your daily waking decision: *I choose joy.*

If you want change, you must completely let go of habits that keep you static. Stop repeating patterns that do not allow you to enact change. Change does not happen unless change is created.

If you want courage, you must fully embrace your bravery. Stand up for yourself, have the critical conversations, do not backpedal, find your warrior, live fiercely.

If you want strength, without fail or frustration, you must attack your weaknesses. With the same level of passion you invest in your strengths, so too must your deficits be addressed.

If you want peace, you must approach all things from a place of calm. A calm that whispers, "I will breathe through this." And with each breath, settle more into your peace. Know that no force or object can move you from that place.

If you want love, you must fully expose your heart. You cannot live guarding against hurt. If you live long enough, if you love big enough, hurt will come to you, for that is the nature of life and love. But if you are willing to reveal your heart's self, that is how love finds you.

If you want anything, you must commit fully to that thing. Until you become that very thing.

Today's life hack.

Less complaining
More celebrating
Less grumbling
More gratitude

Less excuse-making
More results
Less to do
More to be

Less taking
More giving
Less drama
More action

Less fear
More faith
Less quit
More resolve

Less worry
More trust
Less hurry
More patience

Less criticism
More compassion
Less stress
More deep breathing

Less judgment
More acceptance
Less use of emojis
More real emotions

Today's life hack: with less, you have so much more.

If you run long enough . . .

1. You may get lost: But do not panic. Those who dare to wander far most often find themselves well beyond their comfort zone.

2. You may need to catch your breath: But do not stress. While moments of breathlessness are to be treasured, you experience more when you slow to completely inhale and exhale.

3. You may have to slow your pace: But do not fret. While keeping a harried pace, so many must stop. To keep moving forward, that is your goal pace.

4. You may hear the whispers of doubters: But do not pay heed to them. The warriors, the dreamers, the fearless, and the dancers will always be talked about.

5. You may come undone: But do not fear. Being broken is not the worst of things. After the breaking comes the chance to rebuild, reshape, redefine yourself.

6. You may feel like giving in: But do not give over to this. Within you always exists the power of one more—one more mile, one more try, one more day, one more prayer.

If you live long enough.

Did you ever consider that perhaps you're not meant to be handled, because you are more than a handful?

Did you ever consider that perhaps you're not meant to be won, because you are more than a possession?

Did you ever consider that perhaps you're not meant to be fearful of the dark, because you are more than enough light?

Did you ever consider that perhaps you're not meant to be controlled, because you are more than capable of steering your own ship?

Did you ever consider that perhaps you're not meant to be supported, because you are more than strong enough to stand on your own?

Did you ever consider that perhaps you're not meant to be chased, because you are more than a dream?

Did you ever consider that perhaps you're not meant to be given terms and conditions, because you are more than worthy of being loved unconditionally?

Did you ever consider that perhaps you're not meant to be rescued, because you are more than capable of saving yourself?

Did you ever consider that perhaps you are more than?

I do not need you to make me happy
I just want you to share in my joy

I do not need you to try to change me
I just want you to accept me as I am

I do not need you to heal my wounds
I just want you to know there are days I still bleed

I do not need you to plot my course
I just want you to walk with me should I find myself a little lost

I do not need you to move my pain
I just want you to sit still with me should the hurt return

I do not need you to make everything okay
I just want you to hold me until it is

I do not need you to save me from drowning
I just want you to be patient with me as I learn to swim

I do not need you to fix me
I just want you to understand what broke me

I do not need you to try to figure me out
I just want you to embrace the mystery and magic that is me

I do not need you to
But I would love if you just wanted to.

A how-to guide.
How to get ahead
Fall forward
Eyes forward
Keep moving forward
How to overcome
Get up
Step up
Keep your hopes up
How to improve
Make mistakes
Make adjustments
Keep making attempts
How to heal
Choose to let go
Choose acceptance
Keep choosing forgiveness
How to master fears
Turn on the lights
Turn off the doubt
Keep turning toward them
How to be happy
Count your blessings
Count the joy you bring to others
Keep counting the times you are grateful
How to achieve goals
Be patient
Be open to change
Keep being willing to dare
How to treat others
With respect
With kindness
Keep their dignity intact
How to treat yourself
With love
With grace
Keep yourself a priority
How to love
As you hope to be loved
As though it is all you know
Keep it, as ever, unconditional
A how-to guide.

Six common running mistakes:

1. Worrying about where you are not: I have said it before, but apparently it bears repeating. Be where your feet are. Stop stressing about the distant or the distance. Stress steals energy from the moment you are in, the place you currently exist in. Also, while worrying about what may await, you miss the beauty of your current surroundings.

2. Trying to keep up with someone else: Perhaps the greatest mistake you can make is not being true to your own rhythm. And I understand. You are aware of what others are doing. You see what they are accomplishing. But you must understand that it does not reflect poorly on you. Get out of chase mode. Settle into your own pace. You will arrive. And the time will be all yours.

3. Counting down what is left: Counting down leads to *only*—only this more to go, only this much more time to go. Counting up leads to *already*—you've already come so far; you've already put it behind you. *Only* is a clinging to hope. It suggests a need to be done. *Already* is a testament to hope. It suggests a desire to continue.

4. Basing success only on a number: This mistake steals you of celebrations you have a right to acknowledge and to rejoice in. It diminishes accomplishments that are so much greater than a number. When you truly reflect on your most important and valuable achievements, you will see they are not numerical in nature.

5. Playing the "what if" game negatively: Why is it that 99 percent of the time when we ask "what if," it is followed by a negative? *What if I get hurt? What if I fail? What if I can't?* This leads most often to regret. If you are going to play that game, how about you follow it with a positive? *What if I amaze myself? What if I absolutely love it? What if I truly can?* This leads most often to freedom.

6. Overthinking what you do not even have to think about: What we do is simple. We get up, we suit up, we go. But somehow we've made it something much more complicated. We overthink every single thing, right down to our breathing. Get out of your head. You've done this time and time again. You can and will do it again. Just remember to keep it simple, sunshine (KISS). Get up. Suit up. Go.

Six common life mistakes.

Do not worry so much if you come a little undone at the seams; it is how you make room to grow.

Do not worry so much if you fall short of a desired goal; it is how you find out if it is really what you want.

Do not worry so much if you hear the whispers of the doubters; it is how you know who does not belong in your circle.

Do not worry so much if you are made to face your fears; it is how you determine the amount of courage required of you.

Do not worry so much if you must start all over again; it is how you accomplish everything amazing—you begin.

Do not worry so much if you do not have all that you want; it is how you learn gratitude for what you have.

Do not worry so much if you sometimes need to fall completely apart; it is how you discover the parts you want to keep and those you can do without.

Do not worry so much if you do not always have your act together; it is how you come to understand that life is not scripted and you do not need to put on a show for others.

Do not worry so much. It is how you finally give yourself permission to simply be you.

Repeat after me.
I am strong
I am strong when I let go
I am strong when I choose forgiveness
I am strong when I surrender to acceptance
I am brave
I am brave every time I dare to risk
I am brave every time I try once more
I am brave every time I open my heart
I am committed
I am committed to my growth
I am committed to my healing
I am committed to my happiness
I am capable
I am capable of deciding my attitude
I am capable of doing what is best for me
I am capable of controlling my controllables
I am special
I am special for simply being me
I am special for the gifts I possess
I am special for showing others how special they are
I am worthy
I am worthy of respect
I am worthy of my own love
I am worthy of your trust in me
I am disciplined
I am disciplined in habit
I am disciplined in thought
I am disciplined in patience
I am faithful
I am faithful to my faith
I am faithful to my word
I am faithful to my dreams
I am beautiful
I am beautiful in love's eyes
I am beautiful in ways unseen
I am beautiful despite my scars
Repeat after me.
I am.

For a child. For your child. For the child in you.

If you want to be my friend
Please sit in the silence with me
There are times I need you to feel what I cannot say

If you want to be my friend
Please be comfortable with my awkwardness
You see, I am still trying to figure it all out

If you want to be my friend
Please like me when I seem unlikeable
When I am not at my best, it is then I need you more

If you want to be my friend
Please do not fear telling me when I am wrong
I seek truths in all things, but especially in a friend

If you want to be my friend
Please accept our inevitable changes
Everything changes, because everything grows

If you want to be my friend
Please do not get lost in comparisons
Ahead of me, next to me, behind me, I simply want to be able to take hold
of your hand

If you want to be my friend
Please allow me to see your realness
Come to me unfiltered

If you want to be my friend
Please honor the privacy I desperately covet
What happens between hearts stays between hearts

If you want to be my friend
Please offer me your smile
It is the greatest invitation.

Perhaps there should be a few basic rules for running:

1. Do not cheat: It seems simple. Honestly do the work, earn the chance to compete, do not take shortcuts, run all the miles.

2. Run mindfully: Be aware of those around you. Cut off no one, do not be the reason another stumbles or slows, exercise caution and patience when deciding to pass another.

3. Limit the whining: There will always be challenges—poor weather, crowded fields, hills upon hills, the unobservant—none of which you can control. But you can control the amount of whining you do about it.

4. No bashing: Everyone is doing their best. And regardless of how that looks, everyone deserves their spot at the start and to celebrate their finish. There is no need or place for a "better than thou" attitude.

5. The road is open to all: In keeping with #4. You are welcome to this space. It is not reserved for only the elite, the headliners, the first wave. Let us be first to remove the barriers. We all belong. So, lace 'em up, start the clock, be on your way.

Perhaps there should be a few basic rules for living.

A gentle reminder.

If my words do not move you
It is okay to simply move along
Without saying a word

If my thoughts do not fit with yours
It is okay to simply move along
Without throwing a fit

If my stories do not make sense to you
It is okay to simply move along
Without labeling them nonsense

If my goals do not equal yours
It is okay to simply move along
Without discounting them

If my light does not brighten your day
It is okay to simply move along
Without throwing shade my way

If my answers do not pass your test
It is okay to simply move along
Without questioning my decisions

If my steps do not fall in line with yours
It is okay to simply move along
Without leaving a trace

If my love does not help you grow
It is okay to simply move along
Without hating on me

If you do not understand this
It is okay
I will simply move along without you.

I arrived upon your story at the end of every chapter.

. . . and then you decided it was time to rise, so you stood once more.

. . . and then you decided it was time to heal, so you finally forgave.

. . . and then you decided it was time for a change of direction, so you turned and walked away.

. . . and then you decided it was time to be honest, so you let your heart speak for you.

. . . and then you decided it was time to no longer fear, so you simply leapt.

. . . and then you decided it was time to love again, so you began by loving yourself.

. . . and then you decided it was time to start living, so you got on with your life.

I arrived upon your story at the end of every chapter. It told me everything I needed to know.

You may never be 100 percent

. . . ready

. . . courageous

. . . healed

. . . strong

. . . over it

. . . accepted

. . . correct

. . . sure

. . . satisfied

. . . confident

. . . disciplined

. . . patient

. . . okay

You may never be 100 percent.

And that is okay.

Because at 51 percent, you are well on your way.

If you can stop worrying what others think, you will begin to clear cap space for your own thoughts

If you can stop trying to please everyone else, you will begin to better care for your needs

If you can stop comparing your light to that of another, you will begin to see just how brightly you are shining

If you can stop filling yourself with doubt, you will begin making room for hope to fill the empty spaces

If you can stop punishing yourself for past mistakes, you will begin to heal the old wounds

If you can stop desperately clinging to your fear of failure, you will begin to feel it surely slipping away

If you can stop hiding behind your filters, you will begin to realize your beautiful requires no mask

If you can stop waiting to be rescued, you will begin to use your time to become your own superhero

If you can stop, you will begin.

Everywhere I have been, I left behind little pieces of me.

So everywhere I go, I look to replace the missing parts.

And this is how I grow.

Everything real crumbles.

It is the price paid for being real.

Yet among the fragments, beauty remains.

It is the reward for being real.

Those who go in search of peace may never come upon it.

Those who go in peace will find it in all the places they roam.

Your greatest strength exists in the fact that you are in control of your response to adversity, the attitude you possess, the direction your feet are pointed, and the words you speak.

Where there is struggle, there is a chance for learning.

Where there is learning, there is a chance for growth.

Where there is growth, there is a chance for possibilities.

Where there are possibilities, there is a chance for hope.

Where there is hope, there is always a chance.

I got stuck in this place of wanting more. It was its own sort of race, but one I could not win. For there was always more to want. And in that place, there was little room for peace, contentment, or joy. So I took a step away and decided that instead of wanting more, I would work to become more. And my life would be about adding more quality to my days, instead of adding more stuff to my life. My list of things to do now looks a lot different than it used to. And what I found is that I have so much more.

Be more
Kind
Inspired
Disciplined

Think more
Forward
Positively
Beyond your limits

Have more
Faith
Patience
Time for joy

See more
Beauty in others
Good in the world
Than what exists on the outside

Do more
Good
Acts of humanity
Of what gives you goose bumps

Give more
Of yourself
To those in need
Than you can possibly take

Believe more
In yourself
In the process
In the possibilities.

For those who need to speak it.
To those who need to hear it.

If I did not seek your advice
Please offer none

If I did not ask your opinion
Please keep it to yourself

If I did not come to you for input
Please feel no need to shout it out

If I did not want your criticisms
Please do not put them on me

If I did not cause you harm
Please bring none my way

If I did not disrespect you
Please allow me to be me

If I did not appeal to your senses
Please simply look away

If I did not need your guidance
Please take your hands from the wheel

If I did not
Please do not.

I cannot change others
So I focus on improving myself

I cannot control all things
So I handle what is within my power

I cannot make others happy
So I know I am not their source of unhappiness

I cannot predict the events of tomorrow
So I will not waste today's opportunities

I cannot alter events of the past
So I spend little time looking over my shoulder

I cannot stop the hearsay
So I no longer give it my ear

I cannot take back words spoken
So I chose truth, kindness, and heart whispers

I cannot fulfill every expectation
So I find satisfaction in offering my best

I cannot be all things to everyone
So I do not invest my energy there

I cannot
So I gave up trying to.

Fashion tips. What not to wear:

1. The past: It is faded, outdated, no longer your style. And it does not fit anymore.

2. Your button suit: When you wear it, you are simply inviting others to push your buttons. Leave home without it.

3. Envy: Plain and simple, it just doesn't look good on you. Makes you look too small.

4. Other people's shade: That's not your color. Pay them no mind. Keep shining.

5. Excuses like badges of honor: They hang on you. Time to hang them up.

6. Failure like a tattoo: Failing is not permanent ink. It washes off.

7. A fake smile: If you are hurting, you do not need to hide it. Please ask for help.

What not to wear.

This is your pep talk.

Where did you leave your mojo?

Seriously? Is that a real thing?

Really? Oh, okay.

Then let me see if I can help you find it.

Where did you leave your mojo?

Maybe you hid it among all your excuses.

Let's go look there.

Or maybe you tucked it in the drawer where you keep your big-kid pants.

Let's go look there.

Wait, wait, maybe you set it alongside the invitations to your pity party.

Let's go look there.

Still no?

Well, maybe you left it sitting right next to your discipline.

Let's go look there.

Okay, okay, okay.

So I don't really know where you left your mojo, and frankly I'm tired of looking for it.

But the truth is you know where you left it.

It is exactly where you decided to put it down.

Go look there. Then pick it up and get on with it.

You've just been pep-talked.

Training. Not easy to do. But you find a way.

There may be fears to overcome
Not easy to conquer
But you find a way
One small leap at a time

There may be bruises and scars
Not easy to heal
But you find a way
One stitch at a time

There may be reasons to quit
Not easy to keep going
But you find a way
One step at a time

There may be times of doubt
Not easy to believe
But you find a way
One hope at a time

There may be setbacks
Not easy to handle
But you find a way
One get-up at a time

There may be failures
Not easy to accept
But you find a way
One try at a time

There may be heartaches
Not easy to survive
But you find a way
One heartbeat at a time

Living. Not easy to do. But you find a way. One day at a time.

Here's a truth: We get fooled into believing it requires so much energy and so much doing to bring about change, to improve, to make a difference. So much so that it seems impossible or too difficult or simply overwhelming. Therefore, we remain stuck. Paralysis by analysis, as it were. We become lost in the myriad of things we believe we must do. So we often end up doing nothing at all.

The truth is we simply need to do only one thing. And if we can do only that one thing, we would be amazed at how much changes, how much things improve, how much difference we can make. Today I encourage you to find the time, to put forth the effort, to invest your energy in doing your one thing. Pick your one thing. Fully commit to it.

If you can do only one thing
Do your best

If you can do only one thing
Do what you love

If you can do only one thing
Do for another

If you can do only one thing
Do what must be done

If you can do only one thing
Do something different

If you can do only one thing
Do what moves you

If you can do only one thing
Do an act of kindness

If you can do only one thing
Do the good hard work

If you can do only one thing
Do with gratitude

If you can do only one thing
Everything changes.

These are my daily "un" goals.

Unstoppable: I will not permit fears, excuses, distractions, or lack of discipline to keep me from moving forward on my chosen path. I will be relentless in the pursuit of the dreams placed within me.

Unflappable: I will not rant, rage, worry, or escalate over that which I am not in control of. I will not allow my inner peace to be disturbed by the drama and chaos of others.

Understandable: I will clearly communicate my needs without guilt, feeling selfish, or worry of what others may think. I will speak from a place of respect, truth, and love when difficult conversations are required.

Undaunted: I will not allow difficult situations, times, or people to cause me to falter, lose faith, or retreat from my goals. I will not permit the voices of my fears, detractors, or doubts to occupy space in my head.

Unfiltered: I will live in a way that honors and reflects my authentic, genuine self. I will not hide my scars, diminish my light, or stray from my truth. I will be faithful to my nature.

These are my daily "un" goals.

They prevent me from coming undone.

Ten life-changing habits.

And please do not tell me how difficult they are.

1. Focus solely on what you want to achieve, not on what you fear you cannot do.

2. Properly prepare to succeed, as opposed to preparing excuses for why you failed.

3. Do not waver from all that makes you whole, healthy, and happy: insist upon them.

4. Give up three things related to self: self-loathing, self-defeating behavior, self-pity.

5. Discount nothing about yourself: not your worth, not your work, not your goals, not your accomplishments.

6. Have the sense not to give two cents about what others think about you: it is none of your business.

7. Live your life not in comparison or competition with another, for bitterness and loss can be the only by-products.

8. If you must have an attitude, make it one of gratitude: be thankful for everything.

9. Be responsible for the thing you are most responsible for: your own happiness.

10. Fill your life with so much love that there is even enough for you.

Please do not tell me how difficult they are.

Show me how doing them makes living so much easier.

I know it's hard.

Saying no without guilt

Making yourself a priority without feeling selfish

Taking the time to simply rest

Letting go of what hurt you

Forgiving others, forgiving yourself

Walking away from toxic people and places

Stepping into the unknown

Dealing with the criticism

Being truly committed and disciplined

Starting all over

Accepting the wrong that cannot be righted

Facing your deepest fears

Trusting once more

Moving forward alone

Healing the wounded child within you

Picking yourself up again

Loving your imperfections

I know it's hard.

But look where easy got you.

part two: truths

Things I once looked for that I never found.

The easy way out

My happiness in another

Growth without struggle

A valid excuse

Success without failure

The magic pill

Results without the work

A way to change the past

Perfection

Someone to save me

Things I once looked for that I never found, because they do not exist.

The storm could not possibly have known
I am waterproof

The darkness could not possibly have known
I am light-filled

The venomous could not possibly have known
I am anti-venom

The combative could not possibly have known
I am peace-centered

The doubters could not possibly have known
I am faith-driven

The excuses could not possibly have known
I am discipline-based

The demons could not possibly have known
I am warrior-tested

The haters could not possibly have known
I am love-unwavering

They could not possibly have known, or they would not have come calling.

Are you still standing?

Are you willing to keep trying?

Are you fighting to overcome hardships, setbacks, challenges?

Are you striving to do more than survive?

Are you taking steps forward, no matter how small?

Are you working to be the best you possible?

Are you a kind, decent, caring human?

Are you hopeful, grateful, respectful, faithful?

Are you hustling to provide for yourself and those in your care?

Are you modeling self-love for the ones who look to you for love?

Are you giving your love and attention to those you love and attend to?

Are you?

Then you are winning, my friend. You are winning.

There are things I do not care about you.

I do not care how fast you run
I care that you are steady in your resolve to get where you are going

I do not care how far you must go
I care that you refuse to stand still, letting this life pass you by

I do not care what shoes you wear
I care that you never try to fill those of another

I do not care how much you weigh
I care that you do not get so weighed down by your burdens that you forget your blessings

I do not care how much you can lift
I care that you will stop to lift another in need

I do not care if you stood atop the podium
I care that you stood by your word and stood by your friends

I do not care how big your waist is
I care that you are big enough to forgive completely, to dream big, to love again

I do not care how many medals you earn
I care that you earn the trust of a good heart, the respect of the aged and the young, the life you truly want to live

There are things I do not care about you
Because I truly care about you.

These are things you are in control of today:

1. Attitude: So many have fooled themselves into believing their attitude is created by external circumstances. Nonsense. You set your tone.

2. Effort: Few things determine your success in anything more than sheer effort. Be willing to work hard for whatever it is you are after.

3. Outlook: You see what you look at. Read that again. You see what you look at. If you continue looking at all the negative, it becomes all you see. Change your outlook.

4. Words: What you say to yourself matters—always. Why? Because not only do you hear everything you say, you also have grown to believe it. Edit your script. Take out the bullsh*t.

5. Response: Most creatures respond to stimuli on a reflexive level—simply an uncontrolled, programmed response. You are not most creatures. You get to decide how you respond. Here's a tip: make your initial response one of calm.

6. Direction: You have three choices at your disposal: move forward, stay stuck, or take steps backward. While we can debate the benefits of all, only one gets you closer.

7. Time: I realize you cannot alter time. You are, however, in control of what you do with your time. How much time do you spend worrying, wishing, procrastinating, making lists, ranting, arguing, spectating? Imagine if you invested that time toward your goals. Wow.

These are things you are in control of every day. The hardest part is that they remove all your excuses.

Make peace with it:

1. You are going to struggle: When you set your bar high, stuff gets difficult. Make peace with it. It does not mean you can't. It should not lead to frustration. It does not signal weakness. It is a part of the process necessary to move to the next level. Stop complaining about it.

2. You are not for everyone: Not everyone is going to like you. Make peace with it. This life was never meant to be lived as a popularity contest. Nor should you invest time in wondering what others think about you. That is a waste of the precious time you have been given. Stop it.

3. You are fallible: You will make mistakes. You are still learning. Make peace with it. It does not make you a bad person. It makes you human. Forgive yourself, apologize if your mistake caused another harm, then alter your behavior. Stop beating yourself up over it.

4. You are not going to get everything you want: Reality check—just because you want something does not mean it is guaranteed. Make peace with it. You may not win. You may not get the job. You may not capture your unicorn. It does not mean you give up. You reflect, make changes, be patient, recommit. If you want it, you must stop quitting on yourself.

5. You are not in control of everything: Perhaps you realize this, and still you will not let go of trying to. Make peace with it. Frustration, disappointment, and anger are the outcomes of trying to control or change the uncontrollable. It is how and when you become most unsettled. Let it go. Stop the madness.

Make peace with it: the war stops.

Do not be fooled. Not all miles are created equal, because running is hard. Yet you continue.

Some may be all uphill, testing your patience and strength.

Some may not go as planned, a reminder you are not always in control.

Some may be filled with obstacles, each meant to challenge your will.

Some may be traveled in the darkness, bringing to light your deepest fears.

Some may feel hopeless, calling into question your faith.

Some may seem endless, making you want to surrender.

Some may contain roadblocks, forcing you to change course.

Some may require you to go it alone, their own brand of solitary confinement.

Some may break your heart, from which it will be difficult to recover.

Do not be fooled. Not all days are created equal, because living is hard. Yet you continue.

You are free.

You are free to change your mind, your path, your outlook, your direction, your attitude, your circumstances.

You are free to stop fearing what others think, feeling guilty, holding onto the past, allowing others to bring you down, handing over your power, being so hard on yourself.

You are free to go where your heart leads, at your own pace, forward without looking back, a little bit farther, beyond your comfort.

You are free to cancel out the noise, plans that are not in your best interest, your subscription to the drama, memberships to your circle.

You are free to try something new, to better yourself, to try what seems crazy to others, to try the impossible, again and again and again.

You are free to take time for yourself, a step back, a break from the race, care of your needs, off the chains, flight.

You are free to make mistakes, amends, a fresh start, your dream a reality, friends with yourself, peace with the past.

You are free to love unconditionally, once more, as if it is all you know, your one precious life, your own beautiful, amazing self.

You are free.

It comes to this. You have been given a single responsibility: live your life forward.

That is all. Period. Live your life forward.

The mistakes of yesterday. Learn from them. Make changes based off them. Control-Alt-Delete them. Let them go. Live your life forward.

The baggage of yesterday. Leave those bags at the curb. Do not continue to carry them to your new destinations. Put them down. Let them go. Live your life forward.

The wounds of yesterday. Stop allowing them to fester. Seek help for them. Expose them to the air. Heal them. Let them go. Live your life forward.

The failures of yesterday. Do not be defined by them. Do not permit them to influence the effort of today. Grow from them. Let them go. Live your life forward.

The tormentors of yesterday. Give them no more of your power. Remove them from your thoughts. They exist only if you let them in. Let them go. Live your life forward.

The heartbreaks of yesterday. You have survived them all. Every one of them. Feel your heart still beating. Continue to love. Let them go. Live your life forward.

The you of yesterday. Extend grace. Be gentle. Forgive. Embrace. Kiss goodbye. Let go. Live your life forward.

It comes to this. You have been given a single responsibility: live your life forward.

Truths about you that your heart has always wanted you to know:

1. You belong: enter the race, join the club, sign up for the class, take the job, try out for the team, own your place.

2. You cannot be your best friend if you are your own worst enemy: quit discounting, disregarding, disrespecting yourself.

3. You should never measure yourself by any number: Count less of what is countable. What is countless counts more—memories, laughter, adventures, goose bumps, moments of breathlessness.

4. You need never apologize for your song, your dance, your path, your wings, your heart, your life: sing, dance, wander, unfurl, love, live.

5. You are needed: someone wakes up, smiles, has a friend, is loved, because of you.

6. You deserve to be happy, to chase your dreams, to know love, to live your life: you need simply to grant yourself permission.

7. You are beautiful: the discussion ends there.

8. You are more than good enough: right now, just as you are.

9. You, above all else, deserve your own grace, kindness, light, and love: be good to yourself.

10. You possess a superpower: a heart that, even when broken, still beats. A promise that you will be okay.

This is the truth about marathon training:

1. It is times being lost, yet all the while, discovering yourself.
2. It is brokenness and bruises, falling and failing, hurt and heartbreak.
3. It is waking already worn, but rising to accept the challenge.

4. It is beauty and brutality, poetry and pain, artistry and agony.
5. It is demanding, difficult, doable.
6. It is a racing heart, a gasping for air, a sweat broken, a constant pounding.

7. It is wandering in the darkness, toward a light others may not see.
8. It is finding a balance between regiment and rest, risk and reward.
9. It is trying, building, failing, learning, retrying, rebuilding, relearning, growing.

10. It is about evolving and emerging.
11. It is about being real and really being.
12. It is learning to handle both sides of the hill.

13. It is not always rainbows and unicorns.
14. It is maddening, crazy, unpredictable.
15. It is rarely easy.

16. It is continuing despite the struggle.
17. It is overwhelming joy, overcoming pain, overreaching impossibles.
18. It is for the dreamers and believers, the truth seekers and promise keepers.

19. It is but a small amount of time, passing too quickly.
20. It is a chance to give your everything.
21. It is a chance to define yourself.

22. It is not the time between start and finish that most matters, but what you do with the time.
23. It is chasing goose bumps and pursuing breathlessness.
24. It is best approached one day at a time.

25. It is ever worth it.
26. It is, in the long run, about loving the journey.

Scratch that. This is the truth about living.

Truths you may need to hear, truths you may not want to hear:

1. You alone are the creator of your drama: only you have the power to cancel that show.

2. Most of your fears are not based in reality: most of them will never be realized.

3. By wearing your button suit, you encourage others to push your buttons: if you don't wear it, they can't push 'em.

4. You have all the tools to tear down your mountain: you are using them to dig a hole instead.

5. You care too much about what others think: you should think more about what you care about.

6. Blaming others for your problems is easy: the difficulty is that you then must wait for them to solve your problems.

7. You can cling so tightly to your ghost because it requires no strength: it will haunt you until you find strength to let it go.

8. Making excuses does not become you: sooner or later, you become your excuses.

9. No one is coming to rescue you: you possess the power to save yourself.

10. Life is as difficult as you choose to make it: it is also as beautiful as you choose to make it.

Truths you may not want to hear, truths you may need to hear.

Keep your things to do simple.

1. Get up

2. Brush yourself off

3. Tuck yourself in

4. Deep breath

5. Chin up

6. Stand tall

7. Trust yourself

8. Fear less

9. Take a step forward

10. Try again

Keep your things to do simple. Things simply get done.

In order to live a happier, healthier, more productive life, we must move away from our knee-jerk reactions—those easy, readily available responses we have to negative or difficult situations. Our go-to responses, as it were. Here are some reactions that fall into that category, some of which you may reflexively reach for:

1. Worrying: You are so proficient at this that you stay awake at night inventing things to worry about. Let's think of all the ways something could conceivably go wrong. And then let's stress over it. That is energy and time misspent, as most of it never comes to bear and most of it you cannot control.

2. Doubting: You once believed in yourself. Strongly. Deeply. You once had faith in yourself. Unwavering. Abiding. Now, it seems, you have cashed in that belief and faith for nonsense and noise. What the heck? You are grown-ass. Powerful, capable, independent. Act like it.

3. Getting angry: So easy to justify, because "they made me mad." Nonsense. You have a multitude of other responses available. You simply decided to reach for the most convenient one. "But I had a right to be angry." Okay. You also have a right to be calm, silent, bigger than the fight.

4. Ranting: In a world of "warning: long rant ahead," learn to let stuff go. And don't kid yourself; ranting is a form of anger. Doesn't it get exhausting? Here's the thing: Not everything is a thing. Try being less offended by minor offenses.

5. Blaming: See #3. Stop looking around for someone or something to blame. Be responsible for your stuff. Own it. You'll be amazed how life changes when you are completely accountable to and for your words, actions, and results.

6. Discounting: You of the "just" and "only," enough already. This seemingly benign tumor grows cancerous. You begin by discounting your achievements, but it slowly spreads until you start discounting your very worth. Eventually you settle for less than you deserve.

7. Resigning: One of your worst responses. Something gets difficult, and you want to resign from it. Or you begin worrying, doubting, discounting. Interesting how these responses are so intertwined. One way to untangle them: stop quitting on yourself.

8. Apologizing: Saving the worst for last. Stop saying you are sorry for being yourself. You have nothing to apologize for. Not your light. Not your dreams. Not your path. Not your love. Not your life. I'm just sorry for those not able to embrace your brilliant, beautiful, amazing self.

To live a happier, healthier, more productive life, we must move away from our knee-jerk reactions. The next move is yours.

Here is all you need.

Here is all you need to do to succeed: Look past your perceived limits, give up your excuses, move outside your comfort zone. You see, success exists just on the other side of those.

Here is all you need to do to overcome your fear: Take a deep breath, count to three, leap, trust your wings. You see, when you finally face your fear, you realize it has a very short life span.

Here is all you need to do to decrease your stress level: Know your business, handle only the business at hand, mind your own business (what people think of you isn't your business). You see, there is business and there is busyness. Stress results from the latter.

Here is all you need to do during difficult moments: Remember you are strong, remember you are bigger than the moment, remember you have survived every other previous moment. You see, hard times become easier when you remember your truth.

Here is all you need to do to be happy: Count your blessings, the goose bump moments, prayers answered. Add up all the things you are grateful for, all that makes you smile, and all the joys you've known. You see, happiness lies in the ability to take into account what is truly important.

Here is all you need.

And you see, if you do what you need to do, your needs get met.

I had excuses. Life had questions.

This is a life chat.

Me: I will be too old to do that thing.
Life: How old will you be if you don't do that thing? Either way, you will be older.

Me: I am afraid.
Life: Why do you let fear control you? Seems a frightening way to live.

Me: I worry what others will think of me.
Life: What makes you think that somehow matters? Only what you think of you matters.

Me: This is so difficult.
Life: What is it about easy that so resonates with you? I find that difficult to understand.

Me: I lost my motivation.
Life: You need to be motivated to do what is in your best interest? That is very interesting.

Me: I may fail.
Life: Will that be your first time for that? I've failed to keep count.

Me: I just can't.
Life: How have you let that become an option? I just can't fathom that.

Me: Why aren't you buying my excuses?
Life: I've invested so much in you. I couldn't give two cents for your excuses.

I had excuses.

For you. For a friend. For one in need.

If I whispered, "I believe in you,"
Would you hear it above the doubts screaming in your head?

If I whispered, "Try just once more,"
Would you hear it over the voices telling you to give up?

If I whispered, "You are strong enough,"
Would you hear it instead of the lie that you are not enough?

If I whispered, "Do not be afraid,"
Would you hear it beyond the fears that echo in your mind?

If I whispered, "You are not alone,"
Would you hear it through the loneliest nights?

If I whispered, "Take my hand,"
Would you hear it or would mistrust again ring out?

If I whispered, "I am here for you,"
Would you hear it through the walls you have built around yourself?

If I whispered, "I love you,"
Would you hear it amid the beating of your broken heart?

I whispered.

I believe in you, so try just once more. You are strong enough. Please do not be afraid; you are not alone. Take my hand; I am here for you. I love you.

Did you hear it?

Trust me. I get it.

It looms large before you

It is bigger than you

It is so heavy

It appears at times impossible

It makes you wonder how you'll do it

It isn't easy

It seems too big to handle

Trust me. I get it. That's life.

But here's what you do.

You size it up

You take a deep breath

You believe deeply

You lean into it

You trust your strength

You do not allow it to defeat you

You handle it

Trust you. Go get it.

Things you need not fear:

1. Changing: life is change

2. Happiness: give yourself permission

3. Letting go: your heart will thank you

4. Your light: lose the dimmer switch

5. Saying no: it frees you for your yeses

6. Failings: prerequisites for success

7. Being yourself: like it is your only job

8. Making mistakes: learning in progress

9. Chasing a dream: truly live

10. Self-love: no one can love you more

Fear not things you need.

There are times.

There are times I feel lost
But I will not allow myself to surrender

There are times I hurt
But I will not allow myself to suffer

There are times I struggle
But I will not allow myself to complain

There are times I hear the doubters
But I will not allow myself to believe them

There are times I question my path
But I will not allow myself to turn back

There are times I have my excuses
But I will not allow myself to accept them

There are times I buckle beneath the weight
But I will not allow myself to remain down

There are times I must wander alone
But I will not allow myself to feel lonely

There are times I fail miserably
But I will not allow myself to be defined by it

There are times
It is what I will not allow myself to do that has made all the difference.

I stopped asking for things to be easy, and started preparing myself to handle whatever comes my way.

I stopped hoping everything would be okay, and started realizing that no matter what, I will still be okay.

I stopped conceding my power to others, and started taking control of my life.

I stopped worrying about what others might think of me, and started trusting what I believe about myself.

I stopped complaining when things didn't turn out as I wanted, and started paying attention to how I could improve.

I stopped searching for happiness in nouns (people, places, things), and started looking at happiness as an action verb (do, give, love).

I stopped believing I was unworthy of another's love, and started loving myself completely.

I stopped and started. I stopped and started. I stopped and started. It is how I kept moving forward.

Here are fifteen truths about marathon training:

1. Rarely is it easy.

2. Within it, there exist quiet moments of desperation, triumph, heartache, joy, suffering, peace.

3. It does not always strengthen your character, but it will always reveal it.

4. Some days will challenge you physically, some will challenge you mentally. Either way, the challenge is to find a way.

5. Seldom do excuses pay the bills.

6. Eventually the bill comes due.

7. Failure can result, but it cannot be allowed to be the final result.

8. The goal is achieved by a consistent willingness to do the work.

9. No one can do it for you.

10. You will not come out unscathed; it will hurt, tears will be shed, you will be changed.

11. It seems impossible when you look beyond the simplest and most immediate task: finish this mile.

12. You cannot fake it.

13. No matter how difficult it becomes, return to your reason for continuing.

14. It's all about time: making the time, investing the time, prioritizing your time, making the most of your time.

15. The best approach: remain humble, remain grateful, remain hope-filled.

Here is the truth about marathon training: it's a lot like life.

If you should.

If you should fight
Fight your insecurities

If you should argue
Argue against your "can't"

If you should doubt
Doubt your limits

If you should quit
Quit complaining

If you should fail
Fail to make excuses

If you should rage
Rage against your complacency

If you should fear
Fear never chasing your dream

If you should settle
Settle completely into yourself

If you should fall
Fall deeply in love with your life

If? You should.

If you love me
You can forgive my faults

If you love me
You can sit comfortably in my silence

If you love me
You can stand unafraid of my demons

If you love me
You can be okay that I am not always okay

If you love me
You can wander beside me as I find my way

If you love me
You can see my beautiful despite my flaws

If you love me
You can believe in my improbable dreams

If you love me
You can hear the whispers of my heart

If you love me
You can celebrate me home

If you love me
You can allow me to save myself

If you can
Love me.

If you are going to make it
You must stop faking it
Do the work
Face the fear
Set down the excuses
Address the weaknesses
If you are going to make it
You must begin to heal
Do the difficult
Face the past
Set aside the time
Address the issues

If you are going to make it
You must confront your reality
Do a life inventory
Face the facts
Set yourself in motion
Address what needs changing
If you are going to make it
You must invest energy wisely
Do not fear saying no
Face only the thing at hand
Set clear boundaries
Address priorities

If you are going to make it
You must learn to let go
Do what needs doing
Face the unknown
Set yourself free
Address your needs first
If you are going to make it
You must truly believe
Do the impossible
Face up
Set yourself ablaze
Address all things with faith

You are going to make it . . . you must.

During life's difficult moments, I ask myself:

Can you pick yourself up once again?

Can you simply be okay?

Can you forgive completely?

Can you let it go?

Can you choose healing?

Can you summon the strength?

Can you have the courage?

Can you maintain perspective?

Can you learn something from this?

Can you find a way past this?

Can you stay grateful?

Can you continue to love?

During life's difficult moments, I tell myself:

You can.

I woke.

To a new chance
To do
To give
To love

To a new opportunity
For growth
For change
For learning

To a new challenge
To accept
To overcome
To put behind me

To a new unknown
Without fear
Without doubt
Without hesitation

To a new page
Waiting to be colored
Waiting to be written
Waiting to be lived

To a new day
And I am grateful
And I am blessed
And I am hope-filled

To a new me
Braver
Stronger
Closer

I woke anew.

If you want strength
Accept the struggle
Invite the difficult
Seek the challenge

If you want courage
Walk into the darkness
Face the thing you cannot do
Embrace the trembling

If you want peace
Lower the volume
Eliminate the drama
Exist in the moment

If you want change
Start the ripple
Disrupt the norm
Resist the status quo

If you want love
Be the source
Speak from the heart
Love the person you are

The thing you want
Resides on the other side
Of the actions you take.

Self-defeating behaviors:

1. Trying to please others

2. Letting others set your worth

3. Believing others can save you

4. Waiting for others to make you happy

5. Worrying about what others think of you

6. Thinking that what others say alters your truth

7. Allowing others to determine your mood

8. Holding on while others have let go

9. Shrinking yourself so others will be okay

10. Granting others permission to toy with your heart

Often, self-defeat happens in direct relation to the power you give to others.

This is your pep talk.

You are strong enough
To let go
To pick yourself up
To be your own superhero

You are brave enough
To take the leap
To dare to dream
To risk your heart

You are worthy enough
To not settle
To have it all
To never be discounted

You are blessed enough
To be grateful
To no longer complain
To have been given enough

You are good enough
To belong
To take your place
To look others in the eye

You are perfect enough
To love
To be loved
To feel complete

You are _____ enough
So
Already
More than

You've just been pep-talked.

The bad news.

Hoping does not make you strong

Wishing does not make you fast

Worrying does not make you brave

Complaining does not make you healthy

Stressing does not make you happy

Settling does not make you more

Fearing does not make you better

Quitting does not make you resilient

Comparing does not make you complete

The good news.

Doing what you need to does.

The truth is that I struggle.

I struggle to find my strength. Seemingly always are my weaknesses highlighted.

I struggle to find my rhythm. Seemingly always moving to a slightly different tune.

I struggle to find my way to the other side of my fears. Seemingly always stuck standing before them.

I struggle to find my next level. Seemingly always stalled between the status quo and what it will take.

I struggle to find my confidence, to believe I am capable. Seemingly always in doubt of my ability to overcome.

I struggle with the sheer enormity of living. It isn't easy for me. Never has been. It asks more than I am sometimes able to give. Days when it conquers me. Overwhelms me.

And yet the one constant truth of my life: I have never feared the struggle. I know it is coming.

For my struggles are born from a place where dreams and hopes and light exist.

For my struggles are born from a place where grace and forgiveness and love collide.

And I refuse to give up on any of those. I have always known, in my heart, they do not come easy.

And so I have learned to embrace the struggle.

And for the struggle, I am the person I always hoped I would become.

If you ask for the truths in my life, these would be among the greatest. They guide me, they hold me accountable, they shape my decisions. These truths define the life I choose to live. They represent my response to any situation, challenge, or obstacle.

1. Life is beautiful.

2. Honesty is best.

3. Respect is earned.

4. Nothing is guaranteed.

5. Effort is reflected in the result.

6. Failure is a learning opportunity.

7. Faith is more powerful than fear.

8. Humility is not a sign of weakness.

9. Happiness is a conscious decision.

10. Light is greater than darkness.

11. Peace is found in forgiveness.

12. Discipline is a master key.

13. Self-care is a necessity.

14. True love is eternal.

15. Hope is a lifeline.

They are my nonnegotiables. These are my greatest truths.

These are ten simple truths about the long run:

1. If you had strength and faith enough to start, you have strength and faith enough to finish.

2. At times the journey will seem easy, at other times painfully difficult. When it is easy, remain humble. When it becomes difficult, remain grateful. Humility makes you more bearable. Gratitude makes everything more bearable.

3. Your physical capacity to endure is proportional to your mental capacity to believe.

4. Motivation may get you out the door, but discipline will bring you back home again.

5. You don't always have to be brave. You just need a little dose of courage when your fear shows up.

6. If it hurts, you are beyond your comfort zone. If you are beyond your comfort zone, you are growing. If you are growing, you are alive and thriving. Welcome the hurt.

7. Hope is trust magnified. Faith is trust in action. Without trust, you cannot hope to see the path ahead. Without trust, you cannot faithfully act upon your dreams. Trust more, worry less.

8. Strength does not evaporate. It is always present. It is simply a well you must dig deeper to drink from. See #1.

9. Take a really good look behind you. What were once your insurmountables, what were once your impossibles, have been conquered. As you look ahead, it is time you stop doubting yourself.

10. The hills you encounter serve their purposes. To challenge you, to offer you a new view, to lead you to new heights, to allow you the rush of the other side. Never shy away from your hill.

Scratch that. These are ten truths about simply living.

Here is what I have come away with to this point in my journey. I hope these truths make a difference.

1. I am not crazy; I simply see in myself what others may never see. I see a believer, a dreamer, a doer, a humble warrior, a heart bigger than my body gives me credit for. It is easier to believe I am crazy than for others to adjust their lens.

2. Easy is a special brand of poison. While I think I would like this journey to be easy, I have grown to understand that easy never moved me forward. Easy never taught the lesson. Easy never gave me the vision to see what I now see in me. Easy poisons me into believing I need not work hard for what I crave most: personal growth, a dream realized, an unwavering love.

3. Hope, belief, and faith all play a role in what I can achieve. Yet it is faith that matters most. Hope is wanting something to happen. Belief is accepting that something is possible. Faith is the complete trust in this something. I completely trust the dream and my steady resolve to achieve it. Faith.

4. It is launching yourself from the highest cliff that most strengthens your wings. Yet it is the fear of the height that keeps you from spreading your wings. Thus, the apparent dilemma. And the questions mount. To leap? To play it safe? *What if I fail? How will I survive the fall?* But none of this happens if you focus on your singular, greatest truth: You were given wings. End of dilemma.

5. You may not know what awaits you, but you are prepared to handle it. We can never know what is beyond the hill, but for climbing, we are made strong enough to face it. We can never know what is around the bend, but for moving toward it, we are made brave enough to face it. We can never know what challenge will present itself, but for having faith, we are made big enough to overcome it.

6. It is not luck that shall bring you what you seek. It is vision to see what others cannot. Hard work. Faith. Your own wings. And knowing you are enough. Armed with these, luck shall be a bit player in your story.

A difficult but simple truth.

How do you avoid the same potholes along the way?
You do not keep walking down the same street.

How do you stop the voices of doubt from creeping in?
You do not keep listening to the same old soundtrack.

How do you avoid being trapped in a place not meant for you?
You do not keep trying to revisit the past.

How do you stop fear from suffocating you?
You do not keep giving it air to breathe.

How do you keep the demons from winning?
You do not keep engaging them in battle.

How do you allow the wounds to finally heal?
You do not keep tearing off the bandages.

How do you finally come to see your beautiful?
You do not keep viewing yourself through another's lens.

A difficult but simple truth.

Most times, how you do it is by not doing what you keep doing.

The truths.

Addressing your weaknesses
Leads to a path of strength

Facing your fears
Leads to a path of courage

Accepting your challenges
Leads to a path of overcoming

Counting your blessings
Leads to a path of gratitude

Quieting your doubts
Leads to a path of faith

Forgiving yourself
Leads to a path of grace

Eliminating your excuses
Leads to a path of growth

Letting go of your past
Leads to a path of freedom

The truth: you will be led to the path you seek when you take the needed steps.

part three: whispers

quieting the internal noise

. . . the heart's not an organ but a whisper in your head . . .
—John Geddes

Just for today.

I can.

Handle the difficult
Try something new
Embrace my challenges
Continue to make progress
Remain positive in thoughts and actions

I will.

Not fear failure
Accept no excuses
Be solution-oriented
Keep my commitment to myself
Be disciplined in thoughts and actions

I am.

Strong enough
A source of grace
Patient, positive, proactive
Willing to do what is necessary
In control of my thoughts and actions

Just for you.

A stumble is a temporary misstep
Regain your balance, keep dancing

A failure is a temporary mistake
Learn the lesson, make new errors

A fall is a temporary kneel
Say a prayer, rise stronger

A bad mood is a temporary place
Do not get comfortable there, move along

A can't is a temporary mindset
Alter your thoughts, erase apostrophe t

An opportunity is a temporary open door
Decide before it closes, risk or regret

A roadblock is a temporary detour
Find your way around, re-route

A wish is a temporary hope
Establish a plan, make it real

A life is a temporary condition
Do not lose sight of this, love every breath.

Why?

Why does it matter?
Because you matter

Why is it important?
Because you are important

Why should you care?
Because you are cared about

Why not just give up the fight?
Because you are worth battling for

Why take care of the words you speak?
Because you are the story you tell yourself

Why not surrender to that?
Because you are more than this

Why invest the time?
Because you are worth the time

Why push to be your best?
Because you are pulling for yourself

Why continue to try?
Because you are to be continued

Why?
Because you are your why.

What if it was completely broken?
Would you then let it go?

What if it was never meant for you?
Would you then let it go?

What if it was a burden too great?
Would you then let it go?

What if it was holding you back?
Would you then let it go?

What if it was a waste of your precious time?
Would you then let it go?

What if it was not serving your good?
Would you then let it go?

What if it was not contributing to your growth?
Would you then let it go?

What if it was not supposed to be held?
Would you then let it go?

What if you would let it go?

Many go in such a rush
Few go unhurried

Many go looking for a fight
Few go in search of peace

Many go hiding behind a filter
Few go shining their true beauty

Many go never knowing their value
Few go never discounting their worth

Many go fearful of the darkness
Few go carrying their light

Many go wanting it to be easy
Few go willing to accept the difficult

Many go wishing to be motivated
Few go deciding to be disciplined

Many go clinging to their doubt
Few go embracing their faith

Many go lacking a compass
Few go with kindness as their guide

Many go unwilling to risk being broken
Few go understanding love is worth the risk

I need not many to go with me
Only a few.

For you. For a friend. For one in need.

Okay, you told me you failed
Now what will you show me?
Your "gonna quit" or your "try again"?

Okay, you told me you had a bad day
Now what will you show me?
Your "press repeat" or your "put it behind you"?

Okay, you told me you fell
Now what will you show me?
Your "down for the count" or your "get back up"?

Okay, you told me you are in a rut
Now what will you show me?
Your "stay stuck" or your "dig your way out"?

Okay, you told me you got hurt
Now what will you show me?
Your need to suffer or your desire to heal?

Okay, you told me you are afraid
Now what will you show me?
Your "turn and run" or your "face the fear"?

Okay, you told me you have been broken
Now what will you show me?
Your jaded pieces or your "under renovation"?

Okay, you told me life is not fair
Now what will you show me?
Your "I fold" or your "I call your bluff"?

Okay,
Now what?
Your move.

I wish for you a quiet.

A quiet confidence: simply knowing you can, and you will

A quiet strength: simply rising to your feet, every single time

A quiet trust: a whisper that simply says, "I believe in you"

A quiet mind: so you may simply calm your harried thoughts

A quiet moment: to simply slow yourself

A quiet space: so you can simply hear the whispers of your heart

A quiet faith: a silent prayer that simply expresses gratitude

I simply wish for you a quiet.

The keys to happiness:

1. Be thankful: Express your gratitude. If you are busy doing that, you won't have time for your pity party.

2. Stop looking behind you: It's how you miss what's right in front of you. Watch where you're going, not where you've been.

3. Enjoy the little things: Happiness isn't simply found in the big moments of this life. Rather, it exists wherever you allow it.

4. Learn to let go: You hold so tightly to what does not bring you joy. How does that even make sense?

5. Don't use someone else's measuring stick: Quit measuring yourself in comparison to someone else. It is never accurate.

6. Steer your own vehicle: You know where you want to go. Stop letting others mess with your navigational system.

7. Save some love for yourself: You toss that stuff around on everyone else like it's glitter, then want to say how hard it is to love yourself. Please.

The keys to happiness: You own a set. Use them.

The art of flying:

1. Eyes up: you cannot imagine the heights possible if you never set your sights upon them

2. Lighten the load: ditch the excess baggage—your doubts, your fears, your regrets

3. Pack the essentials: faith, perseverance, courage, belief

4. Fear less: leaving the comfortable, stepping off the ledge, the free falling

5. Take calm in the trembling: it is in these moments you realize what you truly want

6. Completely trust: your strength, your wings, your landing

7. Understand: the steps back serve to propel you forward with strength

8. Launch yourself: forward, with hope, toward the dream

9. Learn to glide: not everything needs to ruffle your feathers—know where and when to invest your energy

The art of living.

Dear Friend,

If I said to you, "I am struggling,"

Would you whisper to me, "Give up the fight"?

If I said to you, "I have fallen,"

Would you whisper to me, "It is not worth rising once more"?

If I said to you, "I am so afraid,"

Would you whisper to me, "You are not brave enough"?

If I said to you, "I feel hopeless,"

Would you whisper to me, "All hope is gone"?

If I said to you, "I do not think I can do this,"

Would you whisper to me, "Who are you to even try?"

If I said to you, "I am not beautiful,"

Would you whisper to me, "Hide away in the darkness"?

If I said to you, "I am unworthy,"

Would you whisper to me, "I cannot find value in you"?

If you would not say such things to me,

Then why, dear child, would you ever whisper such things to yourself?

Love,

Me

I am not promised an easy path
So I promise to prepare for a difficult road

I am not promised a successful journey
So I promise to be resilient in defeat

I am not promised everything will turn out right
So I promise to breathe when things go wrong

I am not promised all my goals will be reached
So I promise to celebrate all along the way

I am not promised the days will not grow dark
So I promise to be a source of light

I am not promised how others shall treat me
So I promise to be kind and gentle to myself

I am not promised everything I hope for
So I promise gratitude for all I have

I am not promised the love of another
So I promise to always love myself

I am not promised tomorrow
So I promise to treasure this day

I am not promised anything in this life
So I promise to give it my everything.

To you. To a friend. To one in need.

Dear You,

I want you to know a few things: things you may not know, perhaps forgot, or do not often pay attention to.

Please. Simply read. Do not push aside the words with thoughts or words that contradict what is written. Quiet the noise, both externally and internally.

Please. Simply absorb. Allow the words to settle into the crevices and cracks and open wounds. Let them touch the light in you.

Please. Simply be. Be okay with accepting the words. Do not be quick to discount them. Be open to receiving the truth and gifts contained within.

Within you exists the strength and courage and patience and faith to continue. Oh, I know how weary you get, for the struggle has been great. But once more you took another step—toward healing, toward peace, toward the light. Keep going, my friend. You are going to make it.

Within you lives a light, a magic, a hope, a flame that darkness cannot defeat. Oh, I know you sometimes do not see or feel it, for the storm has been so long. But once more you made it to the light of day. Hold onto hope, my friend. You are going to be okay.

Within you can be found your happiness, your worth, your beautiful, your love. Oh, I know you do not want to believe, for you left these in the hands of others who did not value them. But nothing they could ever do can diminish them. Believe, my friend. You are ever worthy. You are ever beautiful.

Within you has been placed the power to change, to grow, to alter your path, to save yourself. Oh, I know you might fear the power, for change is rarely easy. But when you realize no one is coming to rescue you, you will understand what must be done. Be not afraid, my friend. You are all the superhero you will ever need.

I wanted you to know a few things.

Now you know.

Love, Me

This is my wish for you.

A little less
A little more
Fear a little less
Hope a little more

Worry a little less
Dance a little more
Overthink a little less
Smile a little more

Stress a little less
Trust a little more
Doubt a little less
Believe a little more

Complain a little less
Try a little more
Take a little less
Give a little more

Criticize a little less
Celebrate a little more
Retreat a little less
Shine a little more

Rush a little less
Rest a little more
Regret a little less
Embrace a little more

Settle a little less
Dream a little more
Resent a little less
Love a little more

I wish for you a little less and a little more.

A simple reminder.

Sometimes you simply need to remind yourself exactly who you are.

Feel free to don your cape.

Say, "Hello, beautiful" to the person in the mirror.

Always hold your head up high.

Put on the jacket, show off the medal.

Make "I am so worthy" your mantra.

Dance to the music you hear within your heart.

Step into your own brilliant and amazing light.

Be your own superhero.

Quietly whisper to the universe, "I am the storm."

Sometimes you simply need to remind yourself exactly who you are.

Wishing you a good night.

Tonight, I can.

Let go of this day
Surrender to the rest
Turn down the noise
Release all tensions
Put down my burdens

Tonight, I will.

Dream forward
Take time to just be
Quiet my mind
Stay present
Remember my blessings

Tonight, I am.

Ever hopeful
Grateful for this day
One day stronger
Needed and loved
At peace with myself

This is a good night.

This is a story based on true events.

When I created space for forgiveness
I found an abundance of space for healing

When I created space for my priorities
I found an abundance of time in my day

When I created space for hope
I found an abundance of second chances wanting to be taken

When I created space for belief
I found an abundance of dreams waiting to be captured

When I created space for gratitude
I found an abundance of blessings to give thanks for

When I created space for compassion
I found an abundance of others in need of a soft place to land

When I created space for love
I found an abundance of everything

This is the moral of the story: when you create space, you will find that you have plenty of room.

This is your pep talk. Why not today?

Start over
Start fresh
Start believing
Trust yourself
Trust the process
Trust the journey

Have fun
Have faith
Have fierce goals
Practice smarter
Practice patience
Practice with purpose

Get up
Get going
Get over it
Grow stronger
Grow more gentle
Grow into your dream

Pay attention
Pay it forward
Pay your dues
Spread joy
Spread the word
Spread your wings

Reach out
Reach higher
Reach beyond settling
Let go
Let yourself up
Let love in

Why not today? You've just been pep-talked.

Dear You,

I know you are trying to heal
It is a silent scream
It is a raging out loud
It is a calm and a storm all at once

I know you are trying to recover
It is messy
It is muddy
It is an ugly process

I know you are trying to be brave
It is overcoming darkness
It is stepping into the light
It is courage despite the trembling

I know you are trying to breathe
It is difficult
It is as if there is no air
It is the weight of being held under

I know you are trying to move forward
It is small steps
It is without rhythm
It is an awkward dance

I know you are trying to find your way
It is confusing
It is wandering alone
It is a broken road not found on any map

I know you are trying to put the puzzle together
It is missing pieces
It is pieces that do not fit
It is building a picture without the box

I know. I am trying too.

Love, Me

For you. For a friend. For one who wonders.

Dear You,

I wonder if you know?

I wonder if you know how brave you are?
Despite the doubts, fears, and worries, you have the courage to walk through the darkness. You are brave.

I wonder if you know how strong you are?
Despite the weakness, falls, and failures, you summon the strength to rise every single time. You are strong.

I wonder if you know how special you are?
Despite the loss, heartache, and pain, you find a way to simply forgive. You are special.

I wonder if you know how worthy you are?
Despite the past, the mistakes, and the wrongs done to you, you have remained ever giving. You are worthy.

I wonder if you know how amazing you are?
Despite the broken promises, broken dreams, and broken roads, you remain hope-filled. You are amazing.

I wonder if you know how beautiful you are?
Despite the scars, wrinkles, and tired etched upon you, you possess a loving heart, a gentle spirit, a radiant light. You are beautiful.

Brave. Strong. Special. Worthy. Amazing. Beautiful. This is who you are.

I wonder if you know?

Love,

Me

How do you overcome failure?
You do not stop trying.

How do you overcome darkness?
You do not stop seeking light.

How do you overcome the fear of falling?
You do not stop trusting your wings.

How do you overcome your excuses?
You do not stop to validate them.

How do you overcome feeling defeated?
You do not stop viewing yourself as winning.

How do you overcome the doubts?
You do not stop to feed them.

How do you overcome feeling sorry for yourself?
You do not stop counting your blessings.

How do you overcome heartache?
You do not stop loving.

How do you overcome?
You do not stop.

Maybe, just maybe.

Maybe strength isn't what you lifted, but rather who you lifted. A child. A friend. A stranger in need. Yourself.

Maybe strength isn't a letting go, but rather a holding on. To hope. To a dream. To your tongue. To the hand of a loved one.

Maybe strength isn't a holding on, but rather a letting go. Of yesterday. Of doubt. Of fear. Of what hurt you.

Maybe strength isn't always standing tall, but rather knowing when to take a knee. To pray. To rest. To comfort one who is down. To simply catch your breath.

Maybe strength isn't always rising, but rather not fearing to fall. Completely. Deeply. Hopefully. In love.

Maybe strength isn't a roar to the crowd, but rather a whisper to yourself. *I will be okay. I can do this. I believe in you. I am enough.*

Maybe, just maybe, you possess more strength than you know.

How to lift someone up:

1. Extend to them grace and kindness.

2. Greet them with "Hello, beautiful."

3. Believe in them.

4. Accept them where they are.

5. Offer sincere words of encouragement.

6. Remind them: "You are loved."

7. Do not give up on them.

8. Love them, even as they struggle.

How to lift yourself up.

Life presents itself as a multiple-choice test.

A. Reinforce your excuses
B. Strengthen your resolve

A. Listen to your doubts
B. Quiet the noise

A. Live among your ruins
B. Build yourself a new home

A. Believe your fears
B. Trust yourself

A. Add up your worries
B. Count your blessings

A. Blame everyone else
B. Accept responsibility

A. Hope for motivation
B. Choose discipline

A. Settle for less
B. Know you are worth more

A. Give over to the darkness
B. Be a seeker of light

A. Burden life and love with conditions
B. Live and love unconditionally

A. Wait to be rescued
B. Put on your own cape

A. Sit it out
B. Dance

Life presents itself as a multiple-choice test. Funny thing, you already know all the answers.

So the real question is whether you will make the right choice.

For you. For a friend. For one who needs to know. I thought you should know.

Dear Friend,

I watched as you stumbled along your path
But then I saw you steady yourself
Because I did not look away

I watched as you fell so hard
But then I saw you have the courage to rise
Because I did not look away

I watched as you came unraveled
But then I saw you stitch yourself together
Because I did not look away

I watched as you wandered unknowing
But then I saw you find your way
Because I did not look away

I watched as you sought refuge from the storm
But then I saw you become the storm
Because I did not look away

I watched as you stood trembling at the edge
But then I saw you spread your wings
Because I did not look away

I watched you
Because I could not look away
As you helped me see all that I could become.

Love,

Me

If you were.

If you were ever so very lost
I hope you become a compass

If you were ever in need of a handout
I hope you become a helping hand up

If you were ever wronged
I hope you become a cause for right

If you were ever made to feel different
I hope you become a difference maker

If you were ever frightened by the darkness
I hope you become a lighthouse

If you were ever sinking in hopelessness
I hope you become a vessel for hope

If you were ever treated unkindly and inhumanly
I hope you become an act of human kindness

If you were ever hardened as love took flight
I hope you become a soft place to land

I hope.

I wish.

I wish you no longer wished you were someone different. Who you are, in this moment, is enough. You are worthy.

I wish.

I wish you no longer compared yourself to others. Who you are, as you are, is not lessened by others. You are enough.

I wish.

I wish you no longer viewed yourself as "just." Who you are, all you are, cannot be minimized. You are significant.

I wish.

I wish you no longer allowed yourself to question your gifts. Who you are, all you possess, is valuable. You are special.

I wish.

I wish you no longer worked from a model of deficit. Who you are, what makes you complete, isn't about what you lack. You are whole.

I wish.

I wish you no longer accepted less than you deserve. Who you are, within your heart, is your truth. You are loved.

This is my wish for you.

Failing is not the finish line
You are living proof

Strength is gathered in the struggle
You are living proof

Difficult does not mean impossible
You are living proof

Wounds heal, scars fade, hearts mend
You are living proof

There is always hope
You are living proof

There is always a way through
You are living proof

Miracles happen
You are living proof

Beauty, light, and love exist
You are living proof

Everything will be okay
You are living. Proof.

Comparison is the thief of joy.
—Theodore Roosevelt

Too often, we fall into the trap of comparing our path, our story, our self to that of another—never realizing the damage this habit creates.

As it becomes a vicious cycle of putting ourselves down, feeling like nothing we do is good enough, it leads to further negativity.

Soon we become consumed by want for believing we are somehow lacking. This false void cannot be filled, except with darkness. Joy does not exist there. It lives in the light.

So how do we break this pattern?

Three keys: Perspective. Gratitude. Grace.

Perspective: You must view your life as your own. It stands on its own. You must learn to tell yourself: *This is my path. This is my story. This is me. I am where I am meant to be. No one lived my history. No one holds my tomorrow.*

I am incomparable. That is perspective.

Gratitude: You must be truly thankful for your life. It is filled with opportunities for gratitude. You must learn to pay attention to the many blessings that fill your day. Stop the habit of complaining about what you think you lack. You have enough. You are enough.

I am thankful. That is gratitude.

Grace: You must allow yourself room for forgiveness. You are flawed and imperfect. Beating yourself up for mistakes is a losing game. You cannot defeat the opponent who lives inside you. Let yourself up.

I am human. That is grace.

Perspective. Gratitude. Grace.

With these keys, the door to joy is easily unlocked. And it will come rushing in where it is welcomed.

Be super.

Be super patient
It is in the wait time where you find your answers

Be super kind
It is in the small acts of grace where you find your purpose

Be super forgiving
It is in the letting go where you find your freedom

Be super flexible
It is in the bending where you find you're unbreakable

Be super humble
It is in the quiet belief where you find your greatness

Be super faithful
It is in the trusting where you find your fears dissipate

Be super giving
It is in the unselfishness where you find your cup being filled

Be super loving
It is in the willingness to love yourself where you find your capacity to love another

Be super.

Hey You,

This is for you. It is also probably long overdue. And you may find it somewhat objectionable or offensive, as the language may not be the kind you use. Or it may fall outside of your belief system. Or you simply do not want to hear an unvarnished truth.

To that, I say: Deal with it. Simply take it in and deal with it. You are so absolutely, incredibly amazing! There, I said it. Deal with it.

When on earth did you quit believing and embracing and loving yourself? And why?

Because of something someone said? Because of your past? A scar? A failed relationship? A mistake? Seriously?

Dear sweet child, when will you let it sink in just how beautiful, unique, strong, and blessed you are?

No, I do not want to hear it. I do not want you to sit there, shaking your head, wanting to deny it, telling me how hard it is to believe. Deal with it.

Quit playing small. Quit denying your light. Quit acting as if you have no right to love every single fiber of your being.

Are you not yet weary of carrying around all the junk that does not even belong to you? That someone else made you think you had to hold onto?

You are allowed to put it down, once and for all. Because absolutely no one has permission to steal how you view yourself.

No one has the right to force you to fit within the constructs of their lens.

And 99 percent of the people in your life see you as I do, and you want to fall victim to the 1 percent who simply want to throw shade on you? Please do the math for me on that one.

Let me say it again, and listen up: You are so absolutely, incredibly amazing. Deal with it.

Love,

Me

How to catch a unicorn:

1. Believe in it. If you cannot imagine something or breathe life into it, it never becomes real. But when you truly have faith, you will notice signs of it everywhere. And anything that leaves its mark must surely exist.

2. Practice your technique. Practice, practice, practice. Without true preparation, it will be like trying to lasso the wind. Opportunities do not come often. Perhaps they come only once. Don't be unprepared when you finally get your chance.

3. Approach it slowly. A big mistake is to go rushing toward it. This is not a mistake because it will be frightened (it's been through this before), but rather because you will know fear—a moment of sheer panic when it dawns on you what you are doing. Have patience. Slowly make your way toward it.

4. Persist. No matter how many close calls and near misses, no matter how many failed attempts, do not surrender. By its very nature, the unicorn is elusive. If catching it were easy, everyone would own one. Difficult does not mean impossible. Continue to practice, have patience, learn from previous attempts, try again.

5. Commit to the chase. Be willing to invest the time. Be disciplined in doing the work. Be in it for the duration. Be bigger than your excuses. Be as dedicated to the goal as the goal is dedicated to remaining unattainable. You must win that standoff—every single time.

6. Keep your eyes on the prize. It shines for a reason: so that even during the darkest moments of the hunt, you know it is out there. Keep your head up. It is difficult to hit a moving target. It is nearly impossible if you are always looking down.

No matter what your unicorn, I wish you all the best.

Be the miracle that is life
Breathe
Change
Grow

Be the miracle that is kindness
Give from the heart
Help those in need
Be a source of warmth

Be the miracle that is light
Shine
Light the way
Reflect beauty

Be the miracle that is faith
Believe, truly believe
Follow your heart
Trust what cannot yet be seen

Be the miracle that is time
Have patience
Don't be in a hurry
Slowly unfurl

Be the miracle that is love
Forgive without conditions
Be a source of healing
Act always from a place of peace

Be the miracle that is you
Never surrender your dream
Embrace your uniqueness
Rejoice in who you are right now

Be the miracle.

Dear Child,

Confidence is a fickle and tricky thing to manage, to understand, to gain a sense of. Not easy to gain, quick to evaporate, hard to hold onto. And yet you have every right to be confident in yourself. And you should be. You are a miracle. Let that sink in. You are a miracle.

But as you came to me wanting to know how to gain more confidence, I will offer my simple thoughts. Feel free to take what you need, agree to disagree, or just give it a thought.

It isn't easy, but here is how you grow more confidence:

1. Keep showing up—realize that is a victory. There is much to be said for the warrior who continues to enter the ring. Confidence is not gained when you know you are going to win, nor does it arrive all at once. Confidence is gained when you don't know the outcome, but still you show up and say, "Let's do this." And the bucket slowly gets filled, drop by drop.

2. Keep trying. No matter how hard something gets, do not surrender. Strength is gained in the struggle. As strength grows, so too does confidence. The inverse is also true. As confidence grows, you will begin to see how strong you are becoming. And you will fear less the struggles you are inevitably going to face.

3. Focus on the good, for herein lies your greatest truth: you are special. You have been blessed with talents and thoughts and gifts no one in the entire history of humanity has. Pay attention to these unique and wonderful things about yourself. Then go and be the best you that you can possibly be, whether that is as an athlete, a scholar, or just being a good people. The world needs more good people.

4. Surround yourself with people who want to see you succeed and who believe in you—not simply to have them praise you or celebrate you. These are the people you can trust to be there when you stumble or fail. This will help give you confidence to get up, dust yourself off, and keep going. Show me your friends, and I will show you the path you are heading down.

5. Be gentle with yourself. You hear everything you say about yourself—every single thing. Keep it positive. Stop beating yourself up. Just living this life is hard enough. Do not make it any harder by doubting yourself or speaking poorly of yourself. This is your worst habit. You must be your own best friend. Then talk to yourself like that. You are strong. You are amazing. You are special. Treat yourself as such.

And above all else, know that you are loved.

Love, Me

Believe.

Believe in the infinite possibilities
There is always more than one path

Believe in the dream placed within you
You were gifted it for a reason

Believe in your ability to succeed
You arrived at the start line again today

Believe in the undeniable power of "yet"
Everything you once could not do, you now can

Believe in the healing force that is kindness
Let this be your response to the world

Believe in the steps of your dance
You need not fear stepping on another's toes

Believe in light, hope, and love
Allow them to always guide your choices

Believe in your ability to change your world
Be your own superhero

Believe in the whispers of your heart
They speak an immutable truth

Believe in yourself
Like you believe in someone you love

Believe.

It is never a single thing that does it.

It is always a combination of your choices.

Joy + freedom = love

Patience + trust = goals

Courage + faith = results

Discipline + effort = growth

Trying + learning = success

Resiliency + belief = dreams

Time + forgiveness = healing

Grit + determination = strength

Insistency + consistency = change

Steps forward + steps backward = dancing

Faith: being able to believe what you cannot yet see

Strength: being able to rise after every fall

Gratitude: being able to appreciate what you have

Patience: being able to be where your feet are

Kindness: being able to meet someone where they are

Peace: being able to accept what you cannot control or change

Joy: being able to magnify happiness

Hope: being able to always find the light

Healing: being able to forgive yourself and others

Love: being able to give without conditions

You: a being, able to.

Perhaps you were not gifted with speed
But rather the gift of patience

Perhaps you were not gifted with endurance
But rather the gift of perseverance

Perhaps you were not gifted with strength
But rather the gift of grit

Perhaps you were not gifted with talent
But rather the gift of tenacity

Perhaps you were not gifted with success
But rather the gift of resiliency

Perhaps you were not gifted with courage
But rather the gift of faith

Perhaps you were not gifted with wealth
But rather the gift of abundant gratitude

Perhaps you were not gifted with perfection
But rather the gift of humanity

Perhaps it is not that you have a gift
But rather that you are the gift.

For you. For a friend. For one in need.

Dear You,

I will kneel with you
As you learn to stand once more

I will pick you up from the floor
As you struggle to grow stronger

I will wait for you
As you find your way again

I will pray with and for you
As you remember your faith

I will sit in the darkness with you
As you rekindle your flame

I will believe in you
As you come to trust yourself

I will be okay with the silence in you
As you listen for your heart's whispers

I will hold you in my arms
As you embrace being cared about

I will love you
As you begin to realize you are always worthy

I will be your 3 a.m.
As you face the nothingness

There is but one thing I will not do.

I will not abandon you.

Love, Me

I see 3 a.m. far too often. It is the curse of a daydreamer, a night thinker. It is a piece of being me. One who pays attention to everything. One who hears what others cannot say. One who experiences life as words.

But last night was different. I realized, in the silence and darkness, that there is a nothingness to 3 a.m. And it felt like missing someone.

I know many of you are missing someone in your life. So I tried to put words to what you may not be able to say. And I send my prayers and love to you.

I miss you
In the whispers
Of the falling snow
Of my fading memories
Of an old familiar song

I miss you
In the space
Between inhale and exhale
Between what you left behind
Between the broken pieces

I miss you
In the loneliness
Like an unanswered call
Like a goodbye never spoken
Like these empty arms

I miss you
In the because
Because emptiness has a feel
Because you were a part of me
Because I loved you

I miss you
In the nothingness
That is the silence
That is the darkness
That is 3 a.m.

I miss you.

It is not the leap, it is trusting the landing
This is where faith lives

It is not in the fall, it is in the rising
This is where strength is found

It is not about time, it is about insistence
This is where change occurs

It is not just physical, it is a mental construct
This is where capacity is built

It is not a road many will take, it is still open to all
This is where choice dictates fate

It is not an impossibility, it is an ability to look beyond now
This is where hope grows

It is not always easy, it is a willingness to embrace the struggle
This is where walls come down

It is not what you can do, it is who you become
This is where it all makes sense

It is not "have to," it is "want to"
This is where perspective matters.

I was having a conversation with an amazing and talented young athlete who is afraid of trying out for the basketball team because she does not want to embarrass herself. In her words, she hates when she sucks at stuff.

So, as I usually do, I sat down and I wrote.

Dear Child,

Sometimes they get it wrong.

You should not dance like no one else is watching. You should dance like the whole world is watching.

You should let them see your wings unfurl. And they will know you are capable of taking flight.

You should let them see your stumbles. And they will know it is okay not to be perfect.

You should let them see your tremblings. And they will know courage arrives when you try despite the fear.

You should let them see your beautiful colors. And they will know of all your brilliant shades.

You should let them see you find your rhythm. And they will know you are still learning, still figuring it out.

You should let them see your missteps. And they will know failure and success are just a part of the two-step.

You should let them see your grace. And they will know loving yourself requires that risks be taken.

Just so you know, sweet child, the whole world may be watching, because they are looking to you to know anything is possible. Dance.

Love, Me

This is a story.

You may know of my struggles, but you know not of how much I have already overcome.

You may know of my failures, but you know not of how many times I have risen.

You may know of my miles traveled, but you know not of how I have wandered many a broken road.

You may know of my triumphs, but you know not of how the many losses have shaped me.

You may know of my light, but you know not of how I have trembled alone and afraid in the dark.

You may know of my visible scars, but you know not of how I have been cut so much deeper.

You may know of my brokenness, but you know not of how I have repeatedly stitched myself together.

You may know of my past, but you know not of how my future will unfold.

You may know of my loves lost, but you know not of how greatly I have loved.

You may know of my life, but you know not of how there are days when the living is just hard.

You may know of my name, but you know not of how I came to be who I am.

This is the moral of the story: you may know of me, but it is not the same as knowing me.

Perception vs. reality.

Perception: I possess super strength.
Reality: I simply realize I am always just strong enough.

Perception: I view myself as a superstar.
Reality: I simply do not fear my own light.

Perception: I rely on being super motivated.
Reality: I simply am disciplined in pursuit of my goals.

Perception: I am blessed with super talent.
Reality: I simply work with the gifts I've been given.

Perception: I have supernatural powers.
Reality: I simply pay attention to everything.

Perception: I know a super secret to success.
Reality: I simply will not let failure be my finish line.

Perception: I claim to be superhuman.
Reality: I simply have accepted my imperfections.

Perception: I think I am Superman.
Reality: I simply understand no one else can save me.

In a world of distorted perceptions, I am simply trying to keep it real.

I have come to some conclusions about running:

1. It is hard.

2. Complaining about it doesn't make it easier.

3. It is not complicated: one foot in front of the other.

4. It is not a competition.

5. There is no one "right way" to do it.

6. Eventually it will reveal your character.

7. Success is easy to determine: you are moving forward.

8. Some days you do your best to just survive it.

9. It is okay not to know where it's taking you.

10. Just because it hurts doesn't mean you quit.

11. You should never take it for granted.

12. You should not compare yours to others (see #4).

13. When it is most difficult, it is offering a lesson.

14. It may feel as if it is breaking you, but it is really making you stronger.

15. It is a gift. Treat it as such.

On second thought, I have come to some conclusions about life.

There is something you should know.

Forgive me if I do not remember all the little details as you speak of your day. I was paying attention to all the little details of your face as you spoke.

The way your eyes dance when you talk about love and your loves. The way you bite your lip when you are nervous. The way your smile reminds me of a gentle kiss.

Forgive me if I ask you to repeat yourself over and over. I was paying attention to all the little things that repeatedly amaze me about you.

How your hands tell a story of their own. How you look at me every time as if for the first time. How your laughter is like my favorite song.

Forgive me if I seem distracted when you are near. I was paying attention to all the little nuances of you that make you beautiful.

How kind you are to a passerby. How unaware you are of your light and strength. How you so easily make those around you feel important and special.

Forgive me. It is not that I am not paying attention to anything. You see, I am paying attention to everything.

Maybe I simply view things through a simple lens.

Maybe I simply try to make the difficult seem simple.

Maybe I am too simple to simply understand.

But here is how I look at it.

If you feel stuck, do something about it

If you are not happy, do something about it

If you need a change, do something about it

If you are upset, do something about it

If you want something, do something about it

If you are not where you want to be, do something about it

If you cannot do something, do something about it

If you can do something, do something about it

If you have a dream, do something about it

If you love someone, do something about it

Here is how I look at it.

If you do something about it, maybe something will get done.

You want to speak of weakness when you are strong in so many ways. To keep rising after being knocked down. Strength. To keep fighting when defeat seems imminent. Strength.

You want to speak of emptiness when your life is filled with so many blessings. A brand-new day. Blessing. A beating heart. Blessing.

You want to speak of failure when you have succeeded at so much. You made it through to the light again today. Success. You have not given up. Success.

You want to speak of fear when you are so very brave. You are facing the unknowns. Courage. You are trembling but are willing to leap. Courage.

You want to speak of hopelessness when you have so much to believe in. Your strength. Your blessings. Your successes. Your courage.

Before you speak, listen. And in the pause between hearing and saying, you will know the truth of your life. Speak that.

For you. For a friend. For one in need.

I need you
To fight your demons
Do not succumb to them

I need you
To push back the darkness
Do not let it envelope you

I need you
To put down your weapons
Do not harm yourself

I need you
To ask for help
Do not suffer in silence

I need you
To take my hand
Do not forget I am here

I need you
To know you are priceless
Do not discount yourself

I need you
To speak your truth
Do not fear my response

I need you
To see your beautiful
Do not hide your light

I need you
To be in my life
Do not leave me to wander alone

I need you.

Thought you might need this one.

I am growing
Slowly

I am unfolding
Beautifully

I am changing
Inevitably

I am improving
Daily

I am becoming
Continuously

I am evolving
Amazingly

I am shining
Gently

I am soaring
Fearlessly

I am moving
Faithfully

But if I am not
Still, I am enough.

3 marathons. In 21 days. 78.6 miles. In 11:20:13. That is a lot of time to be inside my head.

Here are 21 random thoughts, simple musings, and mental whispers I processed during that time.

I hope you can apply them to your run, to your life.

1. Even if the crowd is all going the same direction, no one will arrive at your destination.
2. The contest is not against others, but rather with your inner opponents.
3. Your greatest opponent is the one you breathe life into.

4. You vanquish your opponents by doing what they think you cannot.
5. You are either the hunted or the hungry. Stay hungry.
6. Fear is a trespasser. Refuse to give it refuge.

7. Faith is the best companion for your travels.
8. "I can't . . ." is believing something is impossible. It is a lie. "I won't . . ." is believing the lie.
9. You can view pain as a wall or a window. If you choose the former, you cannot see beyond it. If you choose the latter, you know something exists on the other side.

10. Where you are is not as important as where you can see yourself going.
11. What you do after you fail will ultimately determine your success.
12. If every second counts toward your goal, can you afford to waste any of them?

13. Preparation will take you only so far, because nothing can prepare you for everything. Know what you will call on when everything arrives.
14. The mountain is not eroded all at once, but rather one pebble at a time. Persevere.
15. Others can sing your praises, but what you whisper to yourself is always the loudest refrain.

16. Hope is not a recipe for success, but it is a crucial ingredient.

17. Do not pin your hopes on a number. Hang them on something more substantial.

18. What limits you most is not what you believe, but what you do not believe.

19. Not achieving a dream can happen. Not having a dream can never happen.

20. Do not be fooled into thinking those who take the longest are not the strongest. They often carry a burden you do not know.

21. Within you exists the capacity to endure.

If I am special, perhaps it is for attending to the possible within the impossible.

If I am special, perhaps it is that I have faith where others know doubt.

If I am special, perhaps it is for daring to trust my wings when others trust the safety of the ground.

If I am special, perhaps it is because I listen to the whispers of my heart while others pay attention to the noise around them.

If I am special, perhaps it is for keeping my eyes wide open as I dream.

If I am special, perhaps it is not for what I accomplish, but for believing I will accomplish.

If I am special, perhaps it is that I have learned I am capable of saving myself.

If I am special, perhaps it is simply for the loving lens through which you view me.

And that makes you so very special.

You can.

You can rewrite your script

You can be your own superhero

You can go farther than the wall

You can stand atop your Everest

You can be your own brand of great

You can always find the strength needed

You can grow beyond your perceived limit

You can do what it is you set your mind to

You can achieve the dream placed within you

You can succeed at what you've not yet done

You can survive the thing you think will break you

You can.

Call me old-fashioned.

I believe in ladies first
I believe in the Golden Rule
I believe in holding the door
I believe in respecting your elders
I believe in "please" and "thank you"
I believe in chivalry and courtesy

Call me a hopeless romantic.

I believe in love
I believe in goose bumps
I believe in slow dancing
I believe in holding hands
I believe in love everlasting
I believe in fairy-tale endings

Call me foolhardy.

I believe in the power of prayer
I believe few things are impossible
I believe in the resiliency of the heart
I believe you should chase your unicorn
I believe the universe leaves its message
I believe if you leap, your wings will unfurl

Call me a daydreamer.

I believe in dreams coming true
I believe good triumphs over evil
I believe joy is a product of gratitude
I believe in the kindness of strangers
I believe light is greater than darkness
I believe one person can make a difference

Call me what you may.

Just do not say I did not believe.

You have choices available.

Be motivated by self-loathing
Or
Be disciplined by self-love

Criticize and belittle yourself
Or
Cheer for and believe in yourself

Remain within your comfort zone
Or
Remain willing to be uncomfortable

Make excuses for why you will fail
Or
Make plans for how you will succeed

Continue to put your dreams on hold
Or
Continue to hold fast to your dreams

Get upset over things you cannot control
Or
Get up and address the things you can control

View your challenges as being too difficult
Or
View yourself as capable of challenging the difficult

Live your life in fear of what others will think
Or
Live your life independent of what others will think

You have choices available
Or
You have the choice to make some choices unavailable.

I am still trying
To find my way
To find my answers
To find my strength

I am still trying
To undo the chains
To undo the damage
To undo the heartache

I am still trying
To remain brave
To remain patient
To remain hope-filled

I am still trying
To make peace
To make amends
To make a new beginning

I am still trying
To grow into my wings
To grow larger than my fear
To grow beyond my comfort

I am still trying
To stand unbowed
To stand once more
To stand strong in my faith

I am still trying
To love unwavering
To love my imperfections
To love myself completely

So do not worry, my friend, for you see, I am still trying.

Life: it's all take and give.

Take only what you need
Give always more than you take

Take a needed rest
Give yourself a little break

Take time to breathe
Give your breath a chance to catch up

Take nothing for granted
Give your blessings attention

Take the long way home
Give a new path a try

Take stock of your strengths
Give them the steering wheel

Take a leap of faith
Give your wings a little trust

Take very little personally
Give others less emotional control

Take your waking dreams to heart
Give your heart permission to lead

Take a moment for prayer
Give miracles room to exist.

This is an open letter. For a friend. For you. For someone in need.

Dear Friend,

If you are reading this tonight, you were strong enough to conquer the day.
And you will be okay.

If you are reading this tonight, you were much greater than your fears.
And you will be okay.

If you are reading this tonight, you were able to overcome the obstacles.
And you will be okay.

If you are reading this tonight, you were again unstoppable.
And you will be okay.

If you are reading this tonight, you were safely guided beyond the raging currents.
And you will be okay.

If you are reading this tonight, you were not defeated by the battle.
And you will be okay.

If you are reading this tonight, you were not broken by today.
And you will be okay.

If you are reading this tonight, you were previewing your script for tomorrow.
And come the dawn, you will be okay.

Love,

Me

Here are my thoughts on how to train yourself to be mentally tougher:

1. Focus on your controllables. This principle is key to honing your mental toughness. When you bog yourself down with the futile task of trying to control nouns (people, places, things), you not only drain your energy reserve, but you also begin to erode your mental strength as it becomes evident this goal is simply impossible to achieve. On the other hand, in knowing what you can control (attitude, effort, outlook) and investing energy there, you begin to gain power as this goal becomes achievable.

2. Turn down your volume. It is surprising to me what you choose to listen to. So often, you seem to pick the negative frequencies: the doubts, the fears, the perceptions of others, the echoes of your past. Hit the mute button. Or better still, change the channel. You always get to decide what you listen to. Learn to quiet the noise. Choose voices that cheer for you. Speak kindness upon yourself. Even if they are faint whispers, listen for the strains of possibility, of hope, of "I can."

3. Embrace the power of "I am." Nothing is more powerful than the words you put after those two little words—nothing. How you speak of yourself builds or destroys your mental toughness. Sadly, as stated in #2, we so readily reach for words that subtract from our truth, our light, our potential. It is easier to say, "I am afraid" instead of saying, "I am capable of overcoming my fears." The former allows us an out. The latter, however, allows us a chance. Your "I am" is the fuel that powers your mental vehicle.

4. Warrior up—a little tough love for you, sunshine. Warrior up! Whining and complaining and moaning about your circumstances adds nothing to your strength. Quit that habit—immediately. Look at what is before you, make a plan to deal with it, go about the business of getting it done. "Woe is me" is not becoming. It does not flatter you. It is not the way of the warrior. So cinch up your big-kid pants and deal with it.

5. Realize that fear has a life span, and in most cases, it lives for only a few seconds. However, by avoiding your fear, or worse, by feeding your fear, you extend its life span. In most cases, if we simply step

forward and face our fear, we will see a couple of things. First, it typically is not as large as we make it out to be. Second, we usually have to be brave for only five seconds and the fear subsides. And finally, most of what we fear rarely ever comes to pass.

6. Disarm the demon. The only reason your demon puts up a fight is the weapons you provide it. No matter what your demon is, it gains its strength from the weapons you give it. Therefore, until you are ready to disarm it, it is an opponent you cannot defeat. But strip it of its power, and it will surrender to you. Most of our demons reside in our head. But when we practice the five preceding habits, when we become mentally tougher, our demons take up less and less space—until they are no more.

Random thoughts on running a marathon, chasing a dream, living this life:

1. Set a fierce goal: I hear a lot of people say their goal is to "just finish." And while I suspect that is always the ultimate goal, I worry if that is the primary plan, then what is plan B?

2. Have a plan B: If things go astray, as they are apt to do, know what your exit strategy will be. If "just finish" is the goal, the only plan B option is to quit. See why that is an issue? However, if the fierce goal is to finish in fewer than five hours, if things do not go as planned, your exit from that can be to find a way to finish.

3. Shout out the goal: Perhaps modesty keeps us from speaking of the dreams we hold. Or perhaps fear plays a larger role. I imagine many of us fear the possibility of failure (or the perception of failure), and therefore we resist putting it into the universe, never realizing the universe conspires with us when we dare greatly.

4. Rethink failure: So your fierce goal was to finish in sub 5:00, and you achieve a 5:06. Do you really believe you failed? Seriously? Did you hear what I said? You achieved a 5:06! Failure does not exist in achievement. Failure lurks in never daring, never risking, never exposing yourself to the possibility of not reaching a dream.

5. Exit with grace: If you must abandon your fierce goal, do so with grace. Blame no one, offer no excuses, eliminate "should have," "would have," and "could have" from your vocabulary. The simplest way to do this is to simply own your achievement.

6. Commit to your fierceness: To achieve your fierce goal, you must commit to it. Show up, do the work, be prepared to sacrifice, embrace the struggle, learn from setbacks, open yourself to the new and uncomfortable, release fear, be relentless.

7. Believe: Above all, you must believe enough in yourself. In the end, what makes or breaks it is the depth of your belief. With a quiet, humble, unwavering confidence, you will achieve the dreams placed within you. This much you must believe.

Dear Friend,

I pray for you strength
Enough to simply let go
Of anger, of hurt, of sorrow

I pray for you endurance
Enough to completely outlast
The darkness, the struggle, the storm

I pray for you strength
Enough to simply hold on
To light, to hope, to faith

I pray for you endurance
Enough to see beyond this moment
Where there is calm, an exhale, peace

I pray for you strength
Enough to simply be
Without worry, doubt, or fear

I pray for you endurance
Enough to continue
Despite the desire to surrender

I pray for you the strength that comes from enduring the hardships.

I pray for you the endurance that comes from being strong.

Love,
Me

It is difficult for some to walk with me. You see, I am not in a hurry. I feel no rush to become. I am not worried about getting somewhere else. So if you care to walk with me, please be patient.

It is difficult for some to walk with me. You see, I am not into white noise. I feel no need to fill the quiet. I am not worried about the silence that falls around me. So if you care to walk with me, please find comfort in my silence.

It is difficult for some to walk with me. You see, I am not fearful of my struggle. I feel no desire to take the easy path. I am not worried that my wandering will lead me to difficult places. So if you care to walk with me, please understand that it will rarely be without challenges.

It is difficult for some to walk with me. You see, I am not filtered. I feel no pressure to hide my true self. I am not worried if my rawness is too pungent. So if you care to walk with me, please dare to love the real me.

It is difficult for some to walk with me. But you see, because of this, I am now surrounded only by those who have made the choice to remain by my side. Please know I am grateful for your company.

Today's message.

Wake up
Your time is here

Rise up
Above your excuses

Speak up
For what you believe

Lift up
Your words

Reach up
Beyond your comfort

Send up
Prayers of hope

Stand up
You are strong enough

Live up
To your own promise

Love up
On the ones you love

Today's message: there is but one direction.

I am simply going to give myself permission. Permission to crash. To come completely down from the physical and emotional high I have been on for months. I think we so often fear or dread the idea of starting over, starting from scratch. We want to hang onto what we have. We do not want it to be difficult again. And I get that. But as for me, I love the climb. I love the chance to start anew, to rebuild and redefine myself, to apply the lessons I have learned along the way. I love the way getting stronger feels. And so I am giving myself permission to crash.

I am simply going to give myself permission. Permission to take my time. To simply be without fear of missing out. We get that way. Thinking there always has to be something else, something more, something to pursue. We want to see what exists beyond the place we now stand. We do not want to stagnate. And I get that. But as for me, I love the stillness. I love the quiet that comes from turning away from the rush. I love the way healing feels. And so I am giving myself permission to take my time.

I am simply going to give myself permission. Permission to be in awe. To look over my shoulder and marvel at the journey I have taken. We rarely do this, I think for fear of what others may think. We do not want to appear vain or boastful. We seemingly fear looking directly into our own brilliance. We barely dare to whisper, "Wow, I did that." And I get that. But as for me, I love the wonder of the journey. I love knowing it is okay to step into the light. I love the humble soul within in me who also realizes how special I am. And so I am giving myself permission to be in awe.

I am simply going to give myself permission. Permission to not know. To be free to have questions. When did we come to fear not having answers to everything? When did "I have to know" become our mantra? Sure, uncertainty is often uncomfortable. So much of life is about finding our answers. And I get that. But as for me, I love awaking to the fresh, blank page. I love wondering what's behind door #3. I love the goose bumps of the unopened gift. And so I am giving myself permission to not know.

I am simply going to give myself permission. Permission to be human. To let down my guard. To not worry about striving for perfection. To not feel the need to chase the unicorn, the dream. To not have to be "on" all the time. We get caught up in the keeping up. Keeping up with the Joneses. Keeping up the appearances. And I get that. But as for me, I love the Clark

Kent in me. I love eating the cake more than the thought of just having a cake. I love not chasing a thing. I love the off switch. And so I am giving myself permission to be human.

So if you want to know what's next, I am simply going to give myself permission.

Sometimes you are given a chance. What will you do with it?

When you have a chance to pay it forward, you take that chance.

When you have a chance to be there for someone, you show up.

When you have a chance to keep a promise, you make the promise your priority.

When you have a chance to hold another's hopes, you treat them as your own.

When you have a chance to believe in someone, you do not give up on them.

When you have a chance to see someone through the darkness, you remain until the light appears.

When you have a chance to be a hero, you quietly offer your cape to someone else.

When you have a chance to get outside yourself, you find out who you really are.

I view myself through a different lens.

I am not amazing
I am consistently amazed by the gifts and blessings I have been given

I am not inspiring
I am consistently inspired by those I surround myself with

I am not without fears
I am consistently willing to face the fears that reside within me

I am not spectacular
I am consistently unwilling to be a spectator in my own life

I am not motivated
I am consistently disciplined in pursuit of the goals set before me

I am not a machine
I am consistently driven to do the work needed to achieve my dreams

I am not a superhero
I am consistently able to summon the strength and courage within me

I am nothing, if not consistent.

It is quite simple.

Believe, believe, believe
Envision possibilities
Live for the challenge
Insist on discipline
Enjoy the becoming
Visualize success
Escape from comfort

Invest in yourself
Never surrender the dream

You are allowed
Offend your status quo
Unimagine failure

It is quite simple: I believe in you.

Show your mettle

Dare to leap

Trust your wings

Be willing to try again

Raise your ceiling

Question why you fear

Find comfort in discomfort

Assert yourself

Believe in the dream

Chase goals, not ghosts

Get back to your feet

Stop looking behind you

Demand more of yourself

Settle less

Choose kindness

Grow beyond your greatest excuse

Be disciplined

Honor your commitments

Unconditionally love yourself

Show your mettle.

Life asks questions of you.

When your mountain seems insurmountable, will you dare to begin the climb?

When your wall appears suddenly before you, will you dare to find a way around it?

When your fear arrives to stop you from believing, will you dare to keep the faith?

When your path no longer seems clear, will you dare to trust your steps?

When your burden buckles your knees, will you dare to rise to your feet once again?

When your world comes a bit unraveled, will you dare to pull yourself back together?

When your dream demands all you have, will you dare to risk everything?

When your heart knows brokenness, will you dare to continue to love yourself?

Actually, life asks but one question of you: When will you dare?

In a world moving ever quicker, perhaps the secret to success is to be slower.

Slower to anger

Slower to argue

Slower to blame

Slower to complain

Slower to criticize

Slower to doubt

Slower to fear

Slower to get defensive

Slower to hit the panic button

Slower to judge

Slower to nitpick

Slower to offer excuses

Slower to quit

Slower to rage

Slower to rant

Slower to speak

Perhaps the secret to success is to be slower.

Her name is Maria. She may not appear to be a hero, this shy, quiet, diminutive eleven-year-old. This little one with the big fear. She strapped on her harness, tightened her helmet, and slowly climbed her way up the stairs to the gut check some fifty feet above the ground. She made her way to the edge, sat down, and prepared to face her monster. And as she sat there, her classmates below cheered and shouted her name and counted her down. And still, she could not jump. After several agonizing moments, Maria decided she couldn't jump. And she climbed back down the stairs.

However, some fifteen minutes later, there she was again, making that slow climb to the top of the tower. How brave is that? For her monster was no smaller. In fact, perhaps it had grown even larger. This time, the cheers and chants grew larger and louder as her classmates so wanted to see her successfully complete the challenge. But as before, Maria could not bring herself to jump. She climbed back down.

My heart hurt a little for her. I pray for these children's success. I long to see joy within their eyes. She was left to wipe the tears. But I'll be darned if not ten minutes later, there she was again making the climb! And I thought, *Why can't we all be like that?* Why do we give up so easily? Why do we so often back down from the fears and monsters that sit with us?

Here she was, this little one with the giant fear, trying to conquer it yet again. Perhaps the third time really is a charm. And it would make for such a great story if she jumped. But this isn't that story. For a third time, despite the encouragement, applause, and prayers from her friends, she could not bring herself to jump.

And as I watched her slowly make her way down for the final time, I thought her monster was just too big. But we can celebrate her grit and courage to face it time and time again. And so we embraced her. Because that's what we do, we caregivers who want to protect those we care for. And we told her, "It's okay." Because that's what we do, we empaths who want to make everything okay. But as I walked away, I couldn't help but wish that she had jumped. Because that's what we do, we dreamers and seekers and believers in the happy ending.

Moments later, as I stood on the field and watched a pair of students zipping down the zip line, who should I see smiling, screaming, soaring? You guessed it. It was Maria! I threw up both fists, smiled, yelled out, "Woo-hoo, Maria!"

And in that moment, it dawned on me. In the moments when I believed her monster had grown too large, she was simply whittling it down into a more manageable size. When the chance came to finally defeat it, she would. And I thought, *Why can't we all be like that?*

So I leave with this story and hopes that you never forget: Your mountain, your fear, your monster is made smaller each time you decide to face it. Go get to whittling away at it.

I could tell you
You are beautiful
But if you do not see it
My words will fall silently

I could tell you
You are worthy
But if you do not feel so
My words will fall silently

I could tell you
You will be okay
But if you do not trust this
My words will fall silently

I could tell you
You are a gift
But if you cannot accept this
My words will fall silently

I could tell you
You are loved
But if you do not know this
My words will fall silently

I could tell you
I believe in you
But if you do not believe
My words will fall silently

I could tell you
All the words within my heart
But if you do not listen
You will never hear them.

My life does not always follow a plan. Nor does my heart.

There are times I take wrong turns. Travel broken roads. Get lost along the way.

There are times I listen to my heart whisper, "Let's do this."

There are times I color outside the lines. Scribble on the blank pages. Doodle in the margins.

There are times I listen to my heart whisper, "Grant yourself permission."

There are times I push the limits. Explore the boundaries. Discount the impossible.

There are times I listen to my heart whisper, "Why not?"

There are times I make mistakes. Fall ever so hard. Find myself bruised.

There are times I listen to my heart whisper, "You will be okay."

You see, my life does not always follow a plan. Nor does my heart.

For there are times I simply live.

I will fall on my knees for you
If it helps you stand once more

I will walk beside you
If it helps you feel not so all alone

I will patiently wait for you
If it helps you take comfort in your pace

I will sit in silence with you
If it helps you hear your heart's whispers

I will catch you should you fall
If it helps you not fear the leap

I will offer to you my light
If it helps you find a way out of the darkness

I will show you your reflection in my eyes
If it helps you see your beautiful

I will love you when you feel unlovable
If it helps you learn to love yourself

I will. For you.

Love,

Me

When miles seem endless
When miles turn difficult
When miles do not lead home
I shall not weaken

When storms gather
When storms bring darkness
When storms rage
I shall not weaken

When pain comes calling
When pain becomes my companion
When pain is all I feel
I shall not weaken

When burdens mount
When burdens grow heavy
When burdens are all I know
I shall not weaken

When life demands so much
When life seems unfair
When life offers no respite
I shall not weaken

When they whisper, "Give up"
When they whisper, "Quit the fight"
When they whisper, "You cannot win"
I shall not weaken

Now that all of this has made me stronger
I shall not weaken.

I still have my doubts
But I believe more in myself

I still have my weaknesses
But I am strong enough to overcome them

I still have my struggles
But I recognize the growth opportunities they offer

I still have my fears
But I no longer view them through a magnifying glass

I still have my questions
But I am learning to question my answers less

I still have my difficult times
But I do not let them overshadow my moments of breathlessness

I still have my burdens
But I refuse to let them outweigh my blessings

I still have my kryptonite
But I am still capable of being my own superhero.

The challenge is to live fully present, not stressing about what was or what may be.

The challenge is to confront your excuses and fears to understand why you give them air.

The challenge is to rise to the occasion, regardless of the occasion.

The challenge is to completely commit to being better than yesterday.

The challenge is to establish what you want for yourself and never settle for less.

The challenge is to accept, not apologize for, who you are and who you are becoming.

The challenge is to seek, not shy away from, challenges that cause you to grow.

The challenge is to never discount, compare, or surrender to your challenge.

The challenge is to embrace your challenge with a smile, a grace, a humility that simply says, "I've got this."

This is not your grade school show-and-tell.

Tell me not of the excuses you hold
Show me how you will rise above them

Tell me not of what breaks you
Show me how you find the strength to pull yourself together again

Tell me not of this hate-filled world
Show me how you remain a source of unwavering love

Tell me not of how you have been wronged
Show me how you learned forgiveness

Tell me not of what angers you
Show me how you calm the rage within

Tell me not of your shaken faith
Show me how you continue to believe

Tell me not of the fears that paralyze you
Show me how, despite the trembling, you dare to leap

Tell me not of the battles you have lost
Show me how the warrior in you refuses to surrender

Tell me not. Show me how.

This. A story (translated).

You (yes, you!)

Can (as in it is possible)

Do (requires action)

All (even the "impossible")

You (yep, still talking to you)

Hope (the key to all dreams)

When (when? Tell me, when?)

You (it really is about you!)

Finally (isn't it about time?)

And (and, not but)

Simply (keep it simple)

Decide (implies you have a choice)

You (once again, it's up to you)

Will (expressing inevitability)

Trust (an unwavering belief)

Yourself (all parts of you).

If you could see the burdens that weigh me down, perhaps you would offer a helping hand.

If you could see the fears that slow my pace, perhaps you would take the time to walk with me.

If you could see the obstacles I have to overcome, perhaps you would recognize my strength.

If you could see every step forward as a success, perhaps you would celebrate with me.

If you could see the forces that bent me, perhaps you would help me stand tall again.

If you could see the size of my heart, perhaps you would never again judge me by any other measure.

Perhaps, if you would look beyond what you can see, you could just be a little more kind.

It is simple.

Motivation
Or
Discipline ✓

Wishful thinking
Or
Committed action ✓

Standing still
Or
Moving forward ✓

Making excuses
Or
Making progress ✓

Fear-driven
Or
Purpose-driven ✓

Doubt-filled
Or
Hope-filled ✓

Worry-based
Or
Faith-based ✓

Problem-focused
Or
Solution-oriented ✓

Last time I checked, you have a choice.

This is a story.

Perhaps a rhetorical question, perhaps merely the lyrics of a favorite country song, or perhaps something to seriously consider: "Why you hanging on so tight if this ain't working?"

You hang on so tightly
To the past
To your fear
To guilt
Let it go

You hang on so tightly
To the excuses
To your doubts
To grief
Let it go

You hang on so tightly
To the worry
To your untruths
To pain
Let it go

You hang on so tightly
To the wrongs
To your hurt
To anger
Let it go

You hang on so tightly
To the things that are not working
To your script
To uncontrollables
Let it go

This is the moral of the story: a clenched fist seldom solves any problems.

Do not worry that I am pushing myself so hard.
Worry when I no longer care and need to be given a push.

Do not worry that I may fall or fail again.
Worry when I no longer have the courage to try one more time.

Do not worry that I have chosen the path fraught with obstacles.
Worry when I no longer desire to move forward.

Do not worry that I am scarred from life's battles.
Worry when I no longer have anything worth fighting for.

Do not worry that I wear my fragile heart upon my sleeve.
Worry when I no longer am willing to give away my love.

Do not worry that I am seemingly always chasing an impossible dream.
Worry when I no longer believe in the power of my dreams.

Do not worry that I have a plan you just may not understand.
Worry when you care more about what I'm doing than about what you
are doing.

Listen carefully.

Go get today
Expect good things
Try a little smarter

Unlock your heart
Pray for others

Give your best
Extend your friendship
Take a moment to breathe

Use your gifts
Practice patience

Go forward with joy
Enjoy where you stand
Trust yourself

Unplug the negative
Push your boundaries

Get over your "it"
Eyes on the prize
Tell yourself you can

Unclutter your mind
Promise yourself a dream

Life whispers its greatest challenge: "Get up, get up, get up."

In the eyes of others
I may not be seen as special
They simply did not look within my heart

In the eyes of others
I may not be seen as good enough
They simply look at my human imperfections

In the eyes of others
I may not be seen as strong
They simply look in hopes of seeing me fall

In the eyes of others
I may not be seen as worthy
They simply refused to look at me without passing judgment

In the eyes of others
I may not be seen as equal
They simply chose to look through a filter that does not reflect all my colors

In the eyes of others
I may not be seen as beautiful
They simply feared to look directly into my light

In the eyes of others
I may not be seen
They simply do not look at what I can see.

Before the sun rises
The alarm goes off
This is the life of a dreamer

Before the excuses mount
The intentions are set
This is the life of the disciplined

Before the victory is secured
The battle is waged
This is the life of a warrior

Before the light appears
The darkness must be faced
This is the life of a believer

Before the answers are found
The unknown is braved
This is the life of the hope-filled

Before the ache is cured
The heart feels everything
This is the life of an empath

Before the day is ended
The prayers are whispered
This is the life of the grateful

This is the life I choose to live.

You need to be motivated?

To take care of yourself?

To live your best life?

To chase your goose bumps?

To make needed changes?

To get out of your comfort zone?

To do what is right and good?

To give up self-defeating behaviors?

To spend time being healthy?

To be bigger than your excuses?

To pursue your waking dream?

To completely love yourself?

You need to be motivated?

Really?

Interesting.

This is a story.

If you understood your ability to endure, you would fear less the struggle you must face.

If you understood that the opinions of others do not alter your reality, you would fear less what they think.

If you understood that you are priceless, you would fear less having your worth discounted.

If you understood your humanness, you would fear less being less than perfect.

If you understood that your true beauty is a reflection of your inner confidence, you will fear less how the outside world views you.

If you understood that you were given your dreams for a reason, you would fear less making them your life's purpose.

If you understood that you have been gifted this one, precious, finite existence, you would fear less spending your moments in pursuit of what sets you ablaze.

If you understood your capacity to love unwavering, you would fear less giving away the love held within your heart.

This is the moral of the story: In all things, seek understanding. For understanding equals less fear.

Recipe for success.

Respect yourself
Explore alternative methods
Consistently strive for excellence
Insist on discipline
Practice your faith
Expect to succeed

Follow through with your promises
Operate from a place of gratitude
Remember your why

Stay positive
Upset your comfortable
Care less what others think
Constantly seek to improve
Examine your failures
Stop saying "I can't"
Start believing in yourself.

Here's the thing.

If you are looking to take a shortcut, you will most likely end up well short of your intended destination.

If you are looking for the easy way out, you will most likely struggle should the path become difficult.

If you are looking for excuses for why you shouldn't, you will most likely uncover why you didn't.

If you are looking for something to be angry about, you will most likely invent plenty of reasons.

If you are looking for growth without change, you will most likely not grow beyond your comfort zone.

If you are looking for someone else to make you happy, you will most likely search in vain.

If you are looking for a superhero to rescue you, you will most likely end up going down with that ship.

Here's the thing.

If you find yourself lost, most likely you were looking in the wrong direction.

Please do not call me odd for dancing to a song you may not hear.
I am simply moving to the melody of a song still being written.

Please do not call me broken for not having it all together all the time.
I am whole but still human.

Please do not call me antisocial for keeping my circle small.
I am interested in a personal connection in an impersonal world.

Please do not call me selfish for taking care of my needs.
I am able to give only in direct proportion to how healthy I am.

Please do not call me foolish for attempting the impossible.
I am made free for chasing my wild horizons.

Please, do not call me arrogant for holding on to a belief in myself.
I am humble yet aware of my gifts and strengths.

Please do not call me crazy for pursuing a distant dream.
I am merely a dreamer hoping to fully live this one, finite, fragile existence.

If you do not understand, please do not call me.

Love me
Unfiltered
See all my scars, flaws, imperfections
Find my beautiful

Love me
Untethered
Allow me to soar, to dance, to know no cage
Let me use my wings

Love me
Unprejudiced
Accept my history, my storms, my darkness
Embrace the varied hues of me

Love me
Unconditionally
Through the trials, the rising tides, the fire
Remain by my side

Love me
Unwavering
Despite my stumbles, my failures, my doubts
Do not give up on me

Love, Me

Just a thought.

When you check one, you automatically check the other.

No to excuses
Yes to discipline

No to doubt
Yes to faith

No to fear
Yes to courage

No to worry
Yes to trust

No to hurry
Yes to patience

No to negative
Yes to positive

No to whining
Yes to gratitude

No to "woe is me"
Yes to "why not me"

No to comfort zone
Yes to growth zone

No to self-pity
Yes to self-love

Go get today.

part four: lessons

learning to grow

I give thanks to my Creator for this wonderful life
where each of us has the opportunity to learn lessons
we could not fully comprehend by any other means.
—Joseph B. Wirthlin

We can.

We can get over the hump
It is not a mountain

We can begin again this day
It is okay to be a beginner

We can celebrate the victories of others
It does not steal from our own

We can give from a place of gratitude
It is the thankful who have most to offer

We can make a positive difference
It should be on everyone's to-do list

We can share the light within us
It will not diminish our brilliance

We can extend an amazing grace
It is in the forgiving that we heal

We can love as if we've never been broken
It is the shattered who understand love

We can.

Culture is the by-product of consistent behavior.

I am building my culture
Created from faith
A consistent belief that I will succeed

I am building my culture
Created from habit
A consistent routine devoid of excuses

I am building my culture
Created from trust
A consistent knowing it will all be okay

I am building my culture
Created from strength
A consistent power applied to my good

I am building my culture
Created from will
A consistent insistence on discipline

I am building my culture
Created from passion
A consistent need to set myself ablaze

I am building my culture
Created from love
A consistent desire to experience goose bumps

I am building my culture
Created from pillars I consistently reinforce
Faith. Habit. Trust. Strength. Will. Passion. Love.

I have been told, "You make it look easy."

My easy did not happen by making room for excuses, but by making discipline my home.

My easy did not happen by accepting comfortable, but by embracing the moments of discomfort.

My easy did not happen by cursing my burdens, but by using them to strengthen me.

My easy did not happen by never failing, but by never allowing failure to be my stopping point.

My easy did not happen by wishing for an easy path, but by choosing the course wrought with challenges.

My easy did not happen by setting hard limits for myself, but by pushing the boundaries of what I thought possible.

My easy did not happen by fearing what I could not see, but by believing in what I could imagine.

In other words, my easy did not just happen.

Just a thought.

You do not NEED to make it to the top of the mountain.
You need to begin the climb.

You do not NEED to make it to the finish line.
You need to find your way to the starting line.

You do not NEED to be perfect.
You need to embrace your humanness.

You do not NEED to be stronger.
You need to understand you are strong enough.

You do not NEED to be fearless.
You need to find a few seconds of courage.

You do not NEED to see the end of the path.
You need to trust the direction you are headed.

You do not NEED to prove yourself as worthy.
You need to value who you are.

You do not NEED the approval of others.
You need to simply give yourself permission.

You do not NEED to solve all of life's problems.
You need to just conquer today.

Just a thought.

When you do not NEED, your need becomes much easier to fulfill.

It's okay to take a break

From the race
From the noise
From the negative

It's okay to take a break

From your fear
From your doubt
From your worry

It's okay to take a break

From the ache
From the sorrow
From the darkness

It's okay to take a break

From your angst
From your own voice
From your overthinking

It's okay to take a break

From the unknown
From the uncontrollable
From the uncomfortable

It's okay to take a break

From all the things that break you.

You must not fear what must be done.

Moving on
Saying goodbye
Walking away

Owning your story
Seeking your path
Taking back your life

Letting go
Giving up the ghost
Surrendering the past

Failing forward
Trying yet again
Learning from mistakes

Not looking back
Making the ascent
Facing your Everest

The grind
The mundane
The necessary work

Besting the excuses
Overcoming the inertia
Embracing the struggle

Preparing to succeed
Accepting the challenge
Reaching beyond comfort

Seeking goose bumps
Leading with your heart
Following your waking dream

Giving your everything
Living this good, hard life
Loving every piece of yourself.

Perhaps excuses are merely misunderstood.

Perhaps excuses are merely defense mechanisms to keep us from feeling pain.

Perhaps excuses are merely saving graces to keep us from feeling like a failure.

Perhaps excuses are merely nature's remedy to keep us from feeling foolish.

Perhaps excuses are merely acts of self-preservation to keep us from feeling disappointment.

Perhaps excuses are merely safety nets to keep us from feeling fear.

Perhaps excuses are merely protective shields to keep us from feeling love's arrows.

Or perhaps excuses are life's anesthesia meant to keep us from feeling anything at all.

What I thought would break me
Only served to make me stronger

What I thought I could not do
Only made me reevaluate my possible

What I thought I should fear
Only stood as testimony to my courage

What I thought might be my undoing
Only required me to get a grip on myself

What I thought was a fight I could not win
Only asked that I dare to step into the ring

What I thought I could not withstand
Only demonstrated what I can endure

What I thought was too big to handle
Only revealed the true size of my heart

What I thought
Only proved I shouldn't overthink it.

Consider this.

How to face the day, your fears, your struggles in eight steps:

1. Accept what has been handed you—without blame, without resignation, without denial. It is now yours. Do something about it.

2. Stand tall. You do not serve your good when you shrink from your ability, your light, your strengths.

3. Steady yourself. In all things, be balanced. From a solid base, you can launch yourself.

4. Maintain your grip—on your nerve, your faith, your steering wheel.

5. Keep moving. A universal truth is if you just keep moving, you will arrive.

6. Trust—what you know, what you believe, what you cannot yet see.

7. Do not fear the difficult. It is never greater than you; it appears so only if you hand your power over to it.

8. Realize that with every step, with every challenge, with every day, you grow stronger despite how difficult it feels.

Consider this.

Perhaps it is not what you are doing that is holding you back, but rather what you need to stop doing:

1. Stop doubting yourself every time the challenge demands your best.

2. Stop allowing your emotions to be the playground of others.

3. Stop creating excuses when you can be creating solutions.

4. Stop obsessing about things you cannot alter or control.

5. Stop treating yourself like an extra in your life's story.

6. Stop littering your dialogue with the words of regret: *should*, *would*, and *could have*.

7. Stop defending your dreams to those who have not fought the battles with you.

8. Stop discounting your own worth.

9. Stop putting your needs and dreams on hold.

10. Stop believing that completely loving yourself is in any way an act of selfishness.

Perhaps you just need to stop.

Today, I want . . .

to try

to try again

to move

to be moved

to sweat

to sweat fewer little things

to stretch

to stretch my limits

to lift

to lift another

to push

to push beyond comfort

to run

to run right into you

to exercise

to exorcise my demons

to grow

to grow less fearful

Try. Move. Sweat. Stretch. Lift. Push. Run. Exercise. Grow.

Today. I want to.

For a friend. For you. For anyone missing someone.

Amid the missing
May you remember
The joy known
The laughter shared
The memories cherished

Amid the missing
May you remember
The songs sung
The times together
The light they possessed

Amid the missing
May you remember
You can do this
You will be okay
You are not alone

Amid the missing
May you remember
A chance to smile
A reason to celebrate
A life once beautifully lived

Amid the missing
May you remember
Where love once roamed
Forever footprints remain.

A life lesson.

You are strong and capable and worthy.

You are whole and holy and enough.

You are bold and blessed and beautiful.

You are perfectly imperfect and perfectly human and perfectly you.

You are kindness and goodness and awesomeness.

You are growing and learning and becoming.

You are wonder and awe and amazing.

You are light and brilliance and magic.

You are loving and lovable and love.

Lesson: when you recognize all you are, you will begin to love who you are.

A life lesson on strength.

Strength is gathered in facing the difficult. Do the hard work. Take the hard road. Make the hard decisions.

Strength is gathered in the holding on. Cling to hope. Cling to a belief in yourself. Cling to the good in your life.

Strength is gathered in the letting go. Let go of regret. Let go of the past. Let go of all that does not make you better.

Strength is gathered in the push. Push aside your fear. Push past your excuses. Push beyond your comfort.

Strength is gathered in remembering. Remember all the times you stood back up. Remember the dream placed within you. Remember who you are.

Lesson: strength is gathered in the decision to be strong.

For you, my friend.

Hugs. Love. Prayers.

A life lesson on healing.

When trust is broken
Forgiveness heals

When faith is broken
Prayer heals

When the road is broken
Moving forward heals

When hope is broken
Belief heals

When yesterday is broken
Letting go heals

When a dream is broken
Acceptance heals

When a heart is broken
Love heals

Lesson: what is broken can be healed.

A life lesson on dreams.

When you have a dream . . .
You find the time
You make the time
You take advantage of the time

When you have a dream . . .
You find a way
You make a way
You become the way

When you have a dream . . .
You do not make excuses
You do not lean on your excuses
You grow larger than any excuse

When you have a dream . . .
You do what must be done
You do more than what must be done
You do not complain about what must be done

When you have a dream . . .
You believe in the impossible
You believe in what you cannot yet see
You believe in yourself

When you have a dream . . .
You accept the challenge
You accept the difficult
You accept what you are worthy of

When you have a dream . . .
You dare to risk
You dare to fail
You dare to spread your wings

Lesson: when you have a dream, you do more than just dream.

For a child. For your child. For the child in you.

As I prepared my basketball team for their first game of the season, I thought of the message I want to send to them. As I wrote down these items, I realize they do not simply apply to a middle school basketball game. Perhaps you can apply them in your day.

1. Be your own brand of great: You have greatness in you that is not determined by another. Go out and be the best you that you can be.

2. Control your controllables: These include your attitude, effort, and response to adversity. All other things, do not let bother you.

3. Be bigger than the moment: Find a calm within you that allows you not to get overwhelmed in the moment. Especially the difficult moments.

4. Cheer the effort, not the result: Cheering only the results is frequently a path to disappointment. But giving and celebrating the best effort you have takes you down more rewarding paths.

5. Take a lesson from the results: Success teaches us, and failure teaches us. Be open to the lesson and messages each contains.

6. Do not let the results define you: This is one moment, one day. It is not you. You are defined by what a contest or clock or scoreboard cannot measure. Remember that—always.

A life lesson on choice.

You can change it
OR
You can complain about it

You can quit quitting
OR
You can give up

You can trust your wings
OR
You can fear the fall

You can work for it
OR
You can wish for it

You can be kind
OR
You can be critical

You can have results
OR
You can make excuses

You can find the positive
OR
You can search for the negative

You can be your own superhero
OR
You can be a victim of your circumstances

You can treat this life as a gift
OR
You can act as if you're owed something

Lesson: Life is more OR less what you choose.

A life lesson on truth.

Your dream doesn't care where you put your mojo
Your dream cares where your discipline is

Your dream doesn't require inspiration
Your dream depends on perspiration

Your dream doesn't care what you cannot do
Your dream wants to know what you are willing to do

Your dream doesn't want to hear excuses
Your dream wants to see results

Your dream doesn't remember your fall
Your dream is looking for you to get up

Your dream doesn't care if you want to
Your dreams waits to see if you will

Your dream doesn't know it's impossible
Your dream wants to know what you believe

Lesson: sometimes, the truth isn't easy to hear.

A life lesson on stopping.

In a go-go-go world, it is okay to stop.

It is okay to stop feeling guilty for taking care of yourself.

It is okay to stop comparing yourself to others.

It is okay to stop overthinking everything and just let it happen.

It is okay to stop beating yourself up for things you cannot alter.

It is okay to stop holding onto the broken.

It is okay to stop worrying about what others think.

It is okay to stop listening to the noise.

It is okay to stop trying to please everyone.

It is okay to stop accepting less than you are worth.

It is okay to stop pretending everything is okay.

Lesson: It is okay to stop. In fact, at times it is necessary.

A life lesson for a child. For your child. For the child in you.

Simple ways to be a good person.

Share your gifts, your light, your time

Give of yourself, more than you take, without expectation of getting

Take turns, less than you give, nothing that is not yours

Speak kindly, softly, with good intent

Open your eyes, your mind, your heart

Remember the golden rule, please and thank you, what your momma taught you

Offer hope, peace, a safe place to land

Do no harm, your best, good wherever you go

Be kind, honest, mindful of others

Love unwavering, unconditionally, as if it is all that matters

Lesson: It is simple. Be a good person.

A life lesson on attention.

You have my attention.
Therefore, you deserve my time.

You have my attention.
Therefore, you deserve to be greater than my excuses.

You have my attention.
Therefore, you deserve my utmost respect.

You have my attention.
Therefore, you deserve an investment of effort and energy.

You have my attention.
Therefore, you deserve to be attended to daily.

You have my attention.
Therefore, you deserve fidelity and faith.

Lesson: whatever has your attention deserves your best.

A life lesson on choosing.

You get to choose
Your attitude
Your response
Your words

You get to choose
Your path
Your direction
Your pace

You get to choose
Your lens
Your perspective
Your focus

You get to choose
Your joy
Your happiness
Your gratitude

You get to choose
Your worth
Your mindset
Your belief

You get to choose
Your next
Your dream
Your future

You get to choose
Your purpose
Your promises
Your prayer

Lesson: What matters most. You get to choose.

A life lesson on letting go.

Dear Child,

I hope these words reach you.

It will be okay
If you let go of the excuses
In difficult times they become a crutch
If you hobble along without them
It will be okay.

It will be okay
If you let go of the guilt
For what you did or didn't do
If you forgive yourself
It will be okay.

It will be okay
If you let go of the pain
You are not required to carry it
If you allow yourself to heal
It will be okay.

It will be okay
If you let go of the doubts
They serve no value to you
If you begin to believe
It will be okay.

It will be okay
If you let go of the past
What can't change can't come with you
If you simply walk away
It will be okay.

I hope these words reach you.

Lesson: Let it go. You will be okay.

A life lesson on your life.

It is your path
You need not justify where you are headed

It is your challenge
You need not justify how you will overcome it

It is your story
You need not justify the next chapter you are writing

It is your dream
You need not justify why you are chasing it

It is your love
You need not justify who you shall celebrate it with

Lesson: It is your life. You do not need to justify it.

A life lesson on permission.

Dear You,

I have been watching. And wondering.

What is it that keeps you grounded? Tethered to this place?
Do you not know you have wings?

What is it that prevents you from soaring?
And chasing your wildest dreams?
Do you not feel your wings?

What is it that locked your cage door?
Have you simply grown comfortable?
Do you not long to unfurl your wings?

What is it that you so desperately fear?
Is it the height or is it the fall?
Do you not trust your wings?

I have been watching. And wondering.

And I have come to realize it is not about your wings. It is that you've never granted yourself permission to use them.

Lesson: You have always had wings. You have simply needed to give yourself permission to fly.

A life lesson on your words.

If you stop for a moment to consider the power of your thoughts, the weight of your words, perhaps you would wield them more carefully—especially how you use them against yourself.

You see, you hear absolutely everything you think, everything you say. You don't ever miss a word of it. Whether it is merely a thought, a whisper, a scream, you take it all in.

And when your thoughts and words speak negatively of you, it begins to exact a toll upon you. Those constant harsh thoughts and words of doubt begin to erode self-confidence, self-worth, self-realization.

Soon, all the negative words become etched upon the soundtrack of your life. And they begin to determine how you see yourself, how you allow yourself to be treated by others, what you believe you can accomplish, how worthy you feel.

But here's the thing. When you begin to speak to yourself as you do to someone you care about and love, you will notice the change in words, tone, message.

Think of someone you love. A spouse. A partner. A child. A dear friend.

Listen to the genuine compliments you offer them. Pay attention to the words of kindness you direct toward them. Hear the loving words of encouragement, forgiveness, and praise you speak to them.

Why would you not offer yourself the same? You, above all else, deserve such a personal narrative.

Lesson: You hear everything you say. Speak from a place of kindness and love.

A life lesson on control.

There will always be things beyond your locus of control, outside your ability to change. Nouns, for example. People. Places. Things. All uncontrollable. All the time.

We know this. And yet we invest so much energy there until we allow those factors, those uncontrollables, to become our greatest excuses.

Do you ever find yourself saying you were upset or angry because of someone or something outside your control?

Do you ever blame not working out or doing something healthy for yourself on someone or something outside your control?

Do you ever hear yourself talking about having a lousy day because of someone of something outside your control?

It is an easy habit to fall into. Allowing the uncontrollable to become our excuses.

But here's the thing. When we begin to fully invest our energy in what we have complete control over, those excuses will soon fall away.

And there exist three primary areas you always have control over: your attitude, your response, your effort.

Attitude is a choice. And it does not depend on anything or anyone. You have the power to choose and control your attitude.

Your response to any and all situations is always within your control. Always. Because between a stimulus and your response to it, there is always a moment of time for you to decide what you will say, what you will do.

Finally, effort—the greatest power you have. And no one or nothing can diminish it. You are in control. Without excuse.

Invest your energy in that you can control. See how the excuses suddenly are no longer valid.

Lesson: Control your controllables. Everything else will take care of itself.

A life lesson on dreams.

Dreams are interesting things.

It's as if they are a fantasy, and yet they seem so very real.

As children, we believed in the fantasy. We believed in the possibility of our dreams. We acted them out. We pursued them.

We became the heroes within them. We allowed them to be real.

As adults, we seem to no longer believe in the possibility of our dreams. We do not act upon them. We seldom chase them.

We have arrived at a place where heroes are not allowed to exist. We allow dreams to exist only as we sleep.

But here's the thing. It is the dream that makes this life real. That makes us fully awake, fully alive.

The quickening of our pulse. The exhilaration of new. The fear before the leap. The trembling inside. The silent tug in our heart. And oh, those goose bumps.

This is to feel alive.

So chase your dream, my friend. Take that vacation. Write your book. Run that race. Sing your song. Audition for that play. Get your degree. Call that someone. Spread your wings. Climb that mountain. Speak your "I love you." Live that truth. Be your hero.

Lesson: A dream was given to you. It's up to you to make it real.

A life lesson on stopping.

Stop quitting on yourself
Start believing in yourself

Stop doubting yourself
Start trusting yourself

Stop counting your regrets
Start counting your blessings

Stop focusing on the negative
Start paying attention to the positive

Stop complaining about circumstances
Start changing circumstances

Stop lowering your expectations
Start raising your ceiling

Stop listening to your impossible
Start talking about your possibilities

Stop inventing weak excuses
Start creating strong habits

Stop trying to control everything
Start controlling your controllables

Stop stopping
Start starting

Lesson: Life is like that. The more you stop, the easier it is to start.

Twelve don'ts and do's.

For a better today. A better you.

1. Don't act as if today requires more motivation to get through.

2. Do act with discipline and attention toward your goals.

3. Don't allow your excuses room to breathe.

4. Do allow your dreams to consume all the air they need.

5. Don't give credence to the doubters.

6. Do give yourself permission to walk away from them.

7. Don't lose sight of your destination, no matter how far it seems.

8. Do lose the notion that you have failed for not being there yet.

9. Don't place your emotional well-being in the hands of another.

10. Do place an emphasis on being your own emotional caregiver.

11. Don't hold onto guilt, anger, regret, the past, that which cannot be altered.

12. Do hold tightly to acceptance, light, hope, faith, love.

A life lesson on challenges.

There shall come a time when the challenge set before you seems too difficult to overcome. And yet, as you always have, you shall find your way beyond it.

There shall come a time when the challenge set before you conjures up your deepest fears. And yet, as you always have, you shall find the courage needed to quell them.

There shall come a time when the challenge set before you feels as if it is going to break you. And yet, as you always have, you shall be made more complete for having faced it.

There shall come a time when the challenge set before you highlights all your weaknesses. And yet, as you always have, you shall use it to grow stronger.

There shall come a time when the challenge set before you drives you to your knees. And yet, as you always have, you shall rise again to your feet.

There shall come a time when the challenge set before you demands more of you than you believe is possible. And yet, as you always have, you shall achieve your impossible.

Lesson: as always, it is just a matter of time before what challenged you no longer challenges you.

A life lesson on focus.

If you are focused on a number, your focus is too narrow.

If you are focused on a number on your Garmin, your focus is too narrow.

For it cannot measure how far you have truly come. It cannot see how many times you felt like quitting but continued. It cannot describe what it is to walk in your shoes.

If you are focused on a number on the scale, your focus is too narrow.

For it cannot measure your strength, beauty, courage. It cannot see how you are changing from the inside. It cannot describe the love you must have for yourself.

If you are focused on a number on your status, your focus is too narrow.

For it cannot measure who your true friends are. It cannot see the difference you make in the life of another. It cannot describe the power you have to inspire someone else.

If you are focused on a number on the clock, your focus is too narrow.

For it cannot measure the time it takes to achieve a dream. It cannot see the heart needed to find the finish line. It cannot describe who you became for daring to simply start.

Lesson: there is no number that is the measure of you.

A life lesson on if.

If you are still trying
You must have found a reason

If you are still standing
You must have risen once again

If you are still moving
You must have a destination in mind

If you are still struggling
You must have strength left inside

If you are still fighting for yourself
You must have decided you are worth it

If you are still smiling
You must have resolved to be grateful

If you are still grateful
You must have recognized your blessings

If?

Lesson: you must.

This is another life chat. *Jeopardy!* style.

Life: One step at a time
Me: How is the mountain climbed?
Life: This has always been the only way.

Life: One pebble at a time
Me: How is the mountain moved?
Life: If it cannot be climbed, it must be moved.

Life: One light at a time
Me: How is darkness illuminated?
Life: And you must be a source.

Life: One act of kindness at a time
Me: How is the world changed?
Life: A wave begins from the smallest ripple.

Life: One decision at a time
Me: How is my own life changed?
Life: Your next choice alters your path.

Life: One failure at a time
Me: How is success achieved?
Life: Refusing to be defeated is a victory.

Life: One more repetition at a time
Me: How is strength gained?
Life: In all things, to try once more is to become stronger.

Life: One day at a time
Me: How is life best lived?
Life: And it must be this very day.

Life: Understanding the power of one
Me: What is the lesson to be learned?
Life: When you learn this, there shall be nothing you cannot handle, nothing you cannot achieve.

A life lesson on change.

My change came with time
Moments of disappointment
Hours of failure
Days of wondering how and why
Months of trying
Years of growing

My change came with discipline
Moments greater than my excuses
Hours of repetition
Days of doing when I didn't want to
Months of building habits
Years of not counting on motivation

My change came with faith
Moments of believing I could
Hours of knowing I would get there
Days of holding onto hope
Months of trusting the process
Years of holding onto the vision

My change came with hard work
Moments of struggle
Hours of overcoming obstacles
Days of moving beyond comfort
Months of retooling my possible
Years of choosing the difficult path

Lesson: change comes to those with a willingness to change.

A life lesson on strength.

Strength
Of faith
Will lead you
To your knees

Strength
Of hope
Will lead you
To rise once more

Strength
Of discipline
Will lead you
To your goals

Strength
Of character
Will lead you
To do what is right

Strength
Of belief
Will lead you
To success

Strength
Of love
Will lead you
To where you belong

Lesson: Strength has always led you. It shall again.

A life lesson on commitment.

Commitment
When excuses outnumber reasons
And yet you do it anyway

Commitment
When inertia outweighs momentum
And yet you find a way to get moving

Commitment
When failures exceed successes
And yet you do not give up

Commitment
When fears appear greater than courage
And yet you decide to leap anyway

Commitment
When "why bother" is safer than "why not"
And yet you bother to

Commitment
When "don't feel like it" feels better than "feel like it"
And yet you ignore the feels

Commitment
When "just can't" speaks louder than "can"
And yet you listen to the whisper of hope

Lesson: Commitment. When you finally embrace the power of "yet."

A life lesson on need vs. have.

You need not believe an impossible dream
You have to trust all that is possible

You need not always be brave
You have to find just five seconds of courage

You need not play the role of superhero
You have to know you can save yourself

You need not fear being alone
You have to love the company you keep

You need not have all the answers
You have to prioritize your questions

You need not worry what was or will be
You have to stay present in the moment

You need not compare yourself to another
You have to take comfort in being you

You need not protect yourself from love
You have to love as though that is all you know

Lesson: It is not what you need. It is what you have that truly matters.

A life lesson on thinking.

I thought I was to blame
I simply realized I am not another's faults

I thought I could not continue on
I simply had to take the next step

I thought I was of little value
I simply forgot that I determine my worth

I thought I was left all alone
I simply grew to know I am enough

I thought I was robbed of trust
I simply needed to find my faith

I thought I was undeserving of love
I simply understand that this is never the truth

I thought I was completely broken
I simply learned it was letting go of the pieces that no longer fit

Lesson: much of life's troubles are born from simply overthinking it.

A life lesson on the present.

Presently
My goals
Are greater
Than my
Abilities

Presently
My dreams
Are greater
Than my
Possible

Presently
My hopes
Are greater
Than my
Reality

Presently
My fears
Are greater
Than my
Belief

Presently
My doubts
Are greater
Than my
Trust

Presently
My priority
Is to be greater
Than my
Present

Lesson: your present situation is not where you are intended to remain.

A life lesson on life.

Here's what I know about life and I.

It isn't always easy
I did not come here for easy

It isn't always pretty
I am not about how it looks

It isn't always my best
I am just concerned with being better

It isn't always what I hope for
I am making it about what I work for

It isn't always something to write home about
I am still trying to find my way home

It isn't and yet
I am still getting it done.

And in the end, that is all that matters.

Lesson: it isn't always about how you get it done, but that you got it done.

A life lesson on searching.

In your search for perfection
Remember your humanness

In your search for strength
Remember how strong you've been

In your search for forgiveness
Remember to allow yourself grace

In your search for happiness
Remember to enjoy the road

In your search for peace
Remember to just breathe

In your search for change
Remember who you are

In your search for love
Remember to love yourself

Lesson: much is found by simply remembering.

A life lesson on deciding.

Your path is invisible to another
Only you can decide the direction to go

Your story cannot be written by another
Only you can decide the next chapter

Your happiness is not up to another
Only you can decide to experience joy

Your worth does not depend on another
Only you can decide how valuable you are

Your past does not belong to another
Only you can decide to let it go

Your forgiveness is not granted by another
Only you can decide to let yourself up

Your healing is not in the hands of another
Only you can decide to save yourself

Your dream may not be shared by another
Only you can decide to still chase it

Your love may not be accepted by another
Only you can decide you are still and always worthy of being loved

Lesson: Your life. Only you can decide.

A life lesson on counting.

Today I will simply count . . .

Times I express gratitude
Times I fell to my knees
Times I did my best

All my blessings
All my strengths
All my gifts

One more sunrise
One more chance
One more try

Every step forward
Every kind word
Every friend made

The laughs I shared
The smiles I created
The joys I spread

Prayers I send
Hopes I keep
Hugs I give

Fences mended
Limits broken
Promises maintained

Acts of kindness
Acts of faith
Acts of love

Lesson: simply count what really counts.

A life lesson on the small things.

In all things
Small or grand
Remain humble

In all things
Small or grand
Remain patient

In all things
Small or grand
Remain hope-filled

In all things
Small or grand
Remain truthful

In all things
Small or grand
Remain present

In all things
Small or grand
Remain disciplined

In all things
Small or grand
Remain rooted in kindness

In all things
Small or grand
Remain open-minded

In all things
Small or grand
Remain grateful

Lesson: if, in the small things, you can remain true to yourself, the grand things will never make you question who you are.

Today's affirmations. Repeat after me:

1. I am responsible for my emotional well-being. And I will not give this power to someone else.

2. I am worthy of love and happiness. And I will stop discounting this immutable truth.

3. I am able to control my controllables. And I will not allow what I cannot control to control my attitude.

4. I am aware of my inner stature. And I will not play small to appease or build up someone else.

5. I am greater than my fears, excuses, doubts, and failures. And I will no longer define myself by these.

6. I am strong, beautiful, and confident. And I will begin viewing myself only through this lens.

7. I am powerful enough to be my own superhero. And I will not play the role of victim in my life's story.

8. I am filled with gratitude for the blessings in my life. And I will express this in both word and action.

My fears were merely lies whispered over and over when I sat in my darkness.

So I gave up listening to them.

My excuses were merely crutches that kept me from chasing my dreams.

So I gave up leaning on them.

My weaknesses were merely opportunities for me to grow.

So I gave up trying to deny them.

My obstacles were merely stepping-stones to strength.

So I gave up cursing them.

My impossibles were merely illusions created in my doubting mindset.

So I gave up building them.

My past was merely chapters of a story I'm no longer living.

So I gave up trying to rewrite them.

My imperfections were merely my humanness on display.

So I gave up trying to hide them.

My life was merely waiting to begin.

So I gave up waiting for the right time to come along.

Dear Friend,

I don't know how you will summon the strength to carry the burden placed on you. But I know you. And you are strong enough.

I don't know how you will find the courage to face what terrifies you. But I know you. And you are brave enough.

I don't know how you will survive what breaks you in the midnight hour. But I know you. And you are strong enough.

I don't know how you will move beyond your place of despair. But I know you. And you are brave enough.

I don't know how you will rise up and begin once more. But I know you. And you are strong enough.

I don't know how you will calm the anxiety that settles over you. But I know you. And you are brave enough.

I don't know how you will stitch the wound that cannot be healed. But I know you. And you are strong enough.

I don't know how you will fill the emptiness that surrounds you. But I know you. And you are brave enough.

I don't know how you will do what you must do. But I know you. You are strong. You are brave. You are enough.

Love, Me

You do not ever have to like falling short

You do not ever have to like failing to achieve a milestone or dream

You do not ever have to like starting over from scratch

You do not ever have to like your weaknesses being on display

You do not ever have to like being knocked down

You do not ever have to like not meeting your own expectations

You do not ever have to like the difficult path ahead

You do not ever have to like needing to regroup

You do not ever have to like the feeling of being defeated

But you must always love that you again entered the ring to do battle with all you do not like.

Dear You,

I have hopes for you.

I hope the broken road gently leads you where you want to go.
But more than that, I hope you arrive where you are truly wanted.

I hope the winds of change blow gently.
But more than that, I hope that during the storm, you remember your strength.

I hope the mountain ahead gently rises.
But more than that, I hope you do not fear the summit.

I hope the tears fall ever so gently.
But more than that, I hope you always find a reason to smile.

I hope the heartache passes gently with time.
But more than that, I hope you allow your heart to feel again.

I hope the questions come with gentle answers.
But more than that, I hope you find peace in what you know you must do.

I hope the life you are living gently unfolds.
But more than that, I hope that through it all, you treat yourself with grace, kindness, forgiveness, and love.

I gently hope.

Love,

Me

May you wake to a challenge that demands the very best of you.
May you rise to meet it.

May you wake to a voice that whispers, "You are strong, you are beautiful, you are loved."
May it be your own.

May you wake to a path leading you forward.
May it take you where you need to go.

May you wake to a peace of mind.
May it arrive from knowing you can do this once more.

May you wake to a day filled with opportunities to grow, moments to give, chances to take.
May you consume them all.

May you wake to a reason to smile, to express gratitude, to make a difference.
May it be how you greet all who cross your path.

May you wake to a clarity of what you want for your life.
May you relentlessly pursue it.

May you wake to a realization that you are worthy of light, joy, love.
May it change how you treat yourself.

May you wake to a knowing that in the waking, all things are possible.
May you not waste this knowledge on idleness or excuses.

I would rather finish dead last

Than never to have found a reason to start

I would rather struggle against the raging current

Than never to have left the shoreline

I would rather find myself completely broken

Than never to have pushed myself to the breaking point

I would rather collapse under the weight of my own expectations

Than never to have set a goal larger than my current ability

I would rather be devoured by my fears

Than never to have summoned the courage to face them

I would rather fail in pursuit of a dream

Than never to have opened myself to the impossible

I would rather know the heartbreak

Than never to have truly, completely loved.

When you are a dreamer
The days are ever long
The nights are devoid of sleep
For there is much that awakens you

When you are a warrior
The battles are many
The victories seem few
For there is always another dragon

When you are an empath
The places to hide do not exist
The silence rarely ever falls
For there is not a time you do not feel

When you are a wanderer
The roads are always open
The rest stops are far between
For there are miles calling you

When you are a believer
The skeptics are watching
The doubters are simply waiting
For there are those of a shaken faith

When you are an original
The critics will examine you
The masses will search for flaws
For there is a price for being priceless

When you are you
The toll exacted is often great
The investment is worth the cost
For there is true freedom.

A life lesson on failure.

It is not failure
To be driven to your knees
Knowing you will again rise

It is not failure
To fall short of a goal
Knowing within you exists the power of yet

It is not failure
To chase the impossible
Knowing you expanded your possibles

It is not failure
To experience moments of weakness
Knowing with time you gather strength

It is not failure
To turn and walk away
Knowing sometimes it is the right direction

It is not failure
To lose the battle
Knowing it took courage to enter the fray

It is not failure
To arrive at a place of needing help
Knowing self-care never meant "go it alone"

It is not failure
To break completely apart
Knowing the best parts always remain

Lesson: when you know what failure is not, you will realize you have not failed.

The don'ts and the do's.

Don't give in to the temporary urge to quit

Do give in to the need to gather yourself so you can continue on

Don't fall victim to the excuses, fears, and doubts that exist in your head

Do fall in love with knowing they are not greater than the strength that resides in your heart

Don't try to control what you cannot control

Do try, as best as you can, to control your controllables

Don't develop the habit of comparing your progress, goals, and success to those of others

Do develop the habit of celebrating your growth, effort, and personal victories

Don't feel the need to justify your journey or dreams to those who cannot see your path

Do feel justified in following the course you have set your vision upon

Don't think of setbacks, challenges, and obstacle as failures

Do think of difficulties as opportunities to grow stronger

Don't count regrets, tears, and heartaches that have added up in this life

Do count yourself as grateful and blessed for being given this life

Don't believe you have to pretend everything is okay

Do believe that with time, support, faith, and love, everything will be

Lesson: the slogan should have read, "Just don't do it."

I was raised by a strong and amazing woman who instilled in me a belief that I could be whatever and whoever I wanted to be. But it had nothing to do with the career or profession I wanted for myself. Instead her lessons were about becoming the person I wanted to be, for most of all, she taught me not "who to be" but rather "how to be." These are her greatest lessons.

Be a light
Be a safe harbor
Be a servant leader

Be disciplined
Be determined
Be driven by faith

Be faithful
Be friendly
Be forgiving

Be giving
Be gentle
Be gracious

Be honest
Be humble
Be hope-filled

Be inspiring with your actions
Be impeccable with your words
Be insistent toward your goals

Be observant
Be open to change
Be original and creative

Be polite
Be positive
Be prepared

Be true to yourself
Be thoughtful of others
Be thankful for everything.

These are your affirmations for today.

I believe I am powerful enough to change my attitude, mind, intentions, effort, circumstances

I believe in the power of me

I believe I am worthy of joy, forgiveness, patience, dreams, love

I believe in the value of me

I believe I am strong enough to overcome excuses, doubts, fears, obstacles, setbacks

I believe in the strength within me

I believe I am capable, blessed, valued, special, loved

I believe in me.

This is another life chat.

Me: How will I know if I am to stay the course or change directions?
Life: If it brings you joy, peace, fulfillment, walk this path.

Me: And if it does not?
Life: If it brings sorrow, turmoil, discontentment, turn and silently move in a new direction.

Me: How will I know if I am to cling to it or let it go?
Life: If it offers hope, replenishes you, gives you goose bumps, hold it close to your heart.

Me: And if it does not?
Life: If it does not serve your good, empties your reservoir, steals your faith, gently open your hand and let it go.

Me: How will I know if I am to bear the weight or set it down?
Life: If it makes you stronger, prepares you for the journey, does not feel like a burden, place it on your shoulders.

Me: And if it does not?
Life: If it weakens you, holds you back, burdens you with shame, guilt, or doubt, it is not yours to carry.

Me: How will I know if I am to try once more or call it a day?
Life: If it is a dream you see as you wake, if you believe in it, if your heart still whispers, "Yes," you do not quit.

Me: And if it does not?
Life: If you no longer see tomorrow in it, if it does not believe in you, if it no longer calls your name, the story has been written.

Me: But my basic question remains. How will I know?
Life: My dear child, you already know. You must simply find the courage to act in accordance with what you know.

A life lesson on allowance.

Allow yourself
Permission
Opportunities
Freedom
Chances

Allow yourself
Chances to shine
Chances to try new things
Chances to amaze yourself
Chances to make mistakes

Allow yourself
Plenty of mistakes
Plenty of do-overs
Plenty of forgiveness
Plenty of time

Allow yourself
Time to heal
Time to grow
Time to wander
Time to simply be

Allow yourself
To simply be okay
To simply be happy
To simply be present
To simply be you

Lesson: it all begins when you allow yourself.

A life lesson on success.

Be consistent
Show up
Be insistent
Step up

Be consistent
No excuses
Be insistent
No settling

Be consistent
Do the work
Be insistent
Do a little more

Be consistent
Keep moving
Be insistent
Keep improving

Be consistent
Make time
Be insistent
Make the most of your time

Be consistent
Establish habits
Be insistent
Establish priorities

Lesson: success is both a matter of being consistent and insistent.

A life lesson on life.

Envy is not wanting what another has
It is failing to appreciate what you have

Success is not relative to another's journey
It is measured solely by how far you have come

Anger is not caused by another
It is handing over your power to another

Patience is not excusing another's behavior
It is controlling your own

Forgiveness is not dependent on another's actions
It is reliant on how you act toward them

Letting go is not forgetting another's existence
It is the unclenching of your fist so you remember who you are

Happiness is not found within another
It is discovered when you find peace being you

Self-worth is not established by another
It is determined by the love you have for yourself

Lesson: Life is not ever about how another lives. It is the decisions you make about how you want to live.

I thought I was lost
Turns out I was finding my true north

I thought I was failing
Turns out I was preparing to succeed

I thought I was unworthy
Turns out I was unaware of my own value

I thought I was weak
Turns out I was always strong enough

I thought I was not beautiful
Turns out I was viewing myself through the wrong lens

I thought I was never going to get there
Turns out I was taking the time I needed

I thought I was unable to soar
Turns out I was just giving my wings a chance to grow

I thought I was drowning
Turns out I was learning to swim

I thought I was breaking
Turns out I was letting go of pieces that no longer fit

I thought . . .
Turns out I think too much.

A life lesson on being the best version of you.

See the good in another

Offer your hand to another

Speak in gentle tones to another

Teach another

Listen intently to another

Do not judge the path of another

Pray for another

Believe deeply in another

Shine your light for another

Celebrate another

Be patient with another

Allow another their freedoms

Be there for another

Extend grace to another

Love another without condition

Lesson: sometimes being the best version of you isn't really about you.

There is a difference
Between the "want to" and the "will to"

There is a difference
Between tolerance and acceptance

There is a difference
Between telling the truth and being honest

There is a difference
Between an act of kindness and being kind

There is a difference
Between knowing what's right and doing what's right

There is a difference
Between having time and creating time

There is a difference
Between spoken word and silent action

There is a difference
Between a fighter and a warrior

There is a difference
Between needing and wanting

There is a difference
Between simply existing and fully living

There is a difference
Between hoping and believing

There is a difference
Between "love you" and "I love you"

There is a difference.
Be the difference.

A little tough love from your life.

This is an open letter. For you. For a friend. For anyone who needs it.

Hey You,

Yes, you.

What say, just for today, you pull on your big-people pants? You own a pair, yes?

The pair you wear when you want to stop whining and complaining about your current state of affairs and you want to get on with the business of changing what you do not like.

The pair you wear when you are tired of letting what other people say and do and think dictate your emotional well-being, and you want to be responsible for your own happiness.

The pair you wear when you are fed up with making and accepting excuses for why you can't do this or can't do that, and you simply want to get over yourself and just do it.

The pair you wear when you have had enough of being afraid of what others might think of your plans, goals, and dreams, and you decide you are going to finally go for them.

The pair you wear when you decide it is okay to let go of all the useless baggage you carry around that does not serve your good.

The pair you wear when you truly believe you are strong, capable, amazing, beautiful, worthy and deserving of forgiveness, joy, love.

So what do you say? How about it? Go find your big people pants and pull 'em on.

Trust me, they still fit.

Love,

Your Life

This is your pep talk. More or less.

Be more
Need less

Give more
Take less

Do more
Watch less

Listen more
Say less

Breathe more
Rant less

Trust more
Worry less

Smile more
Stress less

Hope more
Complain less

Hug more
Argue less

Forgive more
Fight less

Dream more
Fear less

Love more
Regret less

You've just been pep-talked.

At some point, you have to ask yourself
What are you willing to risk?

At some point, you have to ask yourself
How much do you believe in you?

At some point, you have to ask yourself
When do you decide to live your dream?

At some point, you have to ask yourself
Why have you decided to settle?

At some point, you have to ask yourself
Do you not deserve more?

At some point, you have to ask yourself
Where do you see yourself going?

At some point, you have to ask yourself
What are you waiting for?

At some point, you have to ask yourself
How can you forgive another but not yourself?

At some point, you have to ask yourself
When will you start loving yourself again?

At some point, you have to ask yourself
Why am I so afraid of my answers?

Do you want to know what today will bring? This is your future. This is your fortune.

Today is simply an invitation

To try a little harder

To work a little smarter

To stress a little less

To speak a little kinder

To hug a little tighter

To reach a little higher

To climb a little farther

To become a little better

To breathe a little slower

To forgive a little faster

To dream a little bigger

To stand a little taller

To believe a little deeper

To love a little more

To live a little bolder

So you want to know what today will bring?

All the little things you invite in.

This is your future.

This is your fortune.

I am holding on.

I am holding onto hope
It is my light in the darkest hours

I am holding onto faith
It is my anchor in stormy waters

I am holding onto belief
It is my calm in the chaos

I am holding onto trust
It is my answer in the unknown

I am holding onto kindness
It is my shield in a cruel world

I am holding onto a dream
It is my guide in a deepening fog

I am holding onto unwavering love
It is my strength in this hard life

I am holding onto all that keeps me holding on.

I do not show you my weakness
Not so you think me strong
But so you will not use it against me

I do not show you my deepest pain
Not so you think me invincible
But so you will not do me greater harm

I do not show you my brokenness
Not so you think me unscarred
But so you will not unzip my wounds

I do not show you my kryptonite
Not so you think me a superhero
But so you will not abuse my humanness

I do not show you my stumbles and falls
Not so you think me successful
But so you will not label me a failure

I do not show you my darkness
Not so you think me beautiful
But so you will not dim my light

I do not show you my real self
Not so you think me perfect
But so you will not look away when you see my scars

I will one day show you who I am
Not so you think me different
But so you will understand we are so much the same.

I must remember.

I must have climbed so high
To fall this far
But I must remember
I shall rise again

I must have laughed so loudly
To cry in this silence
But I must remember
I shall smile again

I must have ventured so far
To become this lost
But I must remember
I shall find my way again

I must have flown so freely
To feel this trapped
But I must remember
I shall spread my wings again

I must have been so greatly blessed
To be filled with this emptiness
But I must remember
I shall count my blessings again

I must have lived so joyfully
To know this sadness
But I must remember
I shall feel joy again

I must have loved so deeply
To hurt this hard
But I must remember
I shall love again

I must remember. Again.

This is an open letter.

For you. For a friend. For anyone in need.

Dear Friend,

I cannot promise the pain will end.

I cannot promise there will not be struggles ahead.

I cannot promise the darkness will not come to call once more.

I cannot promise the path shall be easy.

I cannot promise answers to your questions.

I cannot promise the fears shall dissipate.

I cannot promise what was lost shall ever be found.

I cannot promise what I cannot know.

I can promise only that I will be here for you. Always.

And this, I hope you know.

Hugs. Love. Prayers.

The essentials for being successful:

1. Curiosity: Be curious about everything. Ask, try, question, experiment, explore, examine everything. For only in being curious do you open yourself to answers.

2. Focus: on what you focus on. Do you pay attention to what is possible, or do you give your attention (and thus energy) to how difficult the challenge is? In other words, are you solution-oriented or problem-focused?

3. Discipline: the mental switch. Eliminate motivation from the equation. Nothing should ever be about whether you feel like it, whether you want to, or whether you have the motivation to do it. Motivation is not the horse you ride to get to the finish line. Discipline is. Simply do what must be done to get you where you want to be.

4. Faith: in things small and grand. The components of faith include hope, trust, and belief. In every situation, cling to hope. Learn to completely trust yourself. Maintain an unwavering belief in what your heart truly desires.

5. Desire: the passionate pursuit of what you want. Oh, dear child, light yourself ablaze! Comfort, complacency, and contentment are not fuel for living this life. You are meant for so much more. Go. To the places you dream of. Soar. To heights that terrify you. Do. All the crazy, wonderful, beautiful things that call your name. Be. In love with the magic and mystery that is you.

6. Finishing power: Quit quitting on yourself. It's your worst bad habit. In quitting, you fail to realize and utilize your greatest strength: the capacity to endure. You have been divinely created unbreakable. The single greatest truth is that the human spirit is indomitable. Do not give up.

3

The evolution of me.

I learned to be comfortable with being uncomfortable.

I embraced the pain without limit until the pain no longer was my limit.

I was broken to the point of knowing I am now unbreakable.

I never failed to bring myself to the edge of failure.

I gave up giving up on me just because the journey was difficult.

I stopped fearing the fears that caused me to live in fear.

I sat in the silent to hear the whispers only I could hear.

I came to understand that not everyone will understand me.

I accepted that others may never accept me for who I am.

I grew to love myself even as another grew out of love with me.

This is the evolution of me.

So many things to do. Perhaps it is time to undo a few things.

Untie the binds that limit you

Unwind the path that is meant for you

Untangle the cannots that you believe

Unfollow the fears that lead you astray

Unclutter the worry that fills your mind

Unfriend the toxins that feed the negative

Unfurl the wings that you have been given

Unplug the controls that leave you feeling remote

Unmute the whispers that speak to your heart

Unpack the guilts that have become your daily baggage.

My autobiography in eight short chapters.

I leapt
I missed
I fell
I learned

I leapt
I missed
I fell
I tried again

I leapt
I missed
I fell
I grew stronger

I leapt
I missed
I fell
I was humbled

I leapt
I missed
I fell
I rose once more

I leapt
I missed
I fell
I remained hopeful

I leapt
I did not miss
I did not fall
I raised my bar

I leapt
I missed
I fell
I truly lived.

Remember, it is a process.

Purpose establishes priorities

Priorities demand commitment

Commitment requires discipline

Discipline instills consistency

Consistency builds habits

Habits determine success

Success fosters belief

Belief keys confidence

Confidence leads to trust

Trust fosters hope

Hope unleashes faith

Faith precedes love

Love propels you forward.

If I must
I will do this in silence
For in the quiet
There are no critics

If I must
I will do this again and again
For in the trials
There is learning

If I must
I will do this despite the pain
For in the suffering
There is a reservoir of strength

If I must
I will do this consistently
For in the discipline
There is the foundation of habit

If I must
I will do this without complaint
For in the gratitude
There is perspective

If I must
I will do this patiently
For in the passage of time
There is the chance for growth

If I must
I will do this with all my heart
For in the giving of everything
There is the blossoming of love

If I must
I will do this alone
For in the solitude
There is where I shall find me

If I must, I will.

You cannot know all the times I have risen once more to my feet
So judge me not as weak

You cannot know all the fears I have overcome
So judge me not a coward if I am slow to leap

You cannot know all the scars earned for this hard life
So judge me not soft of faith

You cannot know all the miles I have traveled
So judge me not for where I now stand

You cannot know all the blows I have weathered
So judge me not unwilling to face the storm

You cannot know all the doubts I have put behind me
So judge me not a nonbeliever

You cannot know all the times I refused to quit
So judge me not if I stop to catch my breath

You cannot know all the pains my heart has endured
So judge me not if I take time to heal

You cannot know all of me
So judge me not.

It is okay
To raise your bar
But at some point
You have to jump

It is okay
To fear the height
But at some point
You have to jump

It is okay
To catch your breath
But at some point
You have to jump

It is okay
To have your doubts
But at some point
You have to jump

It is okay
To wonder if you can
But at some point
You have to jump

It is okay
To question your strength
But at some point
You have to jump

It is okay
To feel the trembling
But at some point
You have to jump

At some point
You have to jump
But it will be okay.

Because I believed
In myself
In a dream
In the work

Because I did not surrender
To fear
To doubt
To failure

Because I did not listen
To "cannot"
To the cynics
To negative talk

Because I overcame
Excuses
Old habits
Perceived limitations

Because I sought
To grow
To fully live
To challenge myself

Because I would not
Settle
Accept defeat
Give in to "good enough"

Because I was
Disciplined
Determined
Unwavering

Because I simply
Hoped
Trusted
Knew my truth

Lesson: find your because.

Dear Friend,

You are going to be okay.

Perhaps not right now, perhaps not on your time frame, perhaps not for a while. But you are going to be okay.

It is how this life works.

Time, grace, patience, forgiveness, surrender. They all serve to smooth the jagged pieces, lessen the hurt, calm the noise.

You are going to be okay.

Perhaps it doesn't feel like it, perhaps you don't think it will happen, perhaps you can't see how. But you are going to be okay.

It is how this life works.

Light, peace, hope, love. They all remain even in the depths of the darkness, emptiness, and chaos.

You are going to be okay.

Perhaps it will require too much, perhaps it will not be enough, perhaps it will not ever be the same. But you are going to be okay.

It is how this life works.

Hearts heal, wounds close, pain fades. They all are truths that do not change. They simply need to be remembered.

You are going to be okay.

It is how this life works.

Love,

Me

To achieve the goals you want in any area of your life, these are the keys.

Be real intentional
Make decisions with a purpose

Be real disciplined
Do not rely on motivation alone

Be real focused
Keep your attention directed to the goal

Be real honest
Especially with yourself

Be real consistent
Progress requires consistency

Be real brave
Change feels scary, find your courage

Be real committed
Jump with both feet

Be real resilient
Do not be discouraged by setbacks

Be real positive
Negativity erodes

Be real passionate
Lead with your heart

Lesson: to achieve the goals you want, the key is to be real.

Look for the good
In others

Look for the good
In the struggle

Look for the good
In the moment

Look for the good
In the intention

Look for the good
In the change

Look for the good
In the difficult

Look for the good
In the storm

Look for the good
In the setback

Look for the good
In the uncertainty

Look for the good
In the new

Look for the good
In yourself

Lesson: what you look for, you will see.

These are the gifts I give myself. These are the gifts I wish for you.

Courage
To be myself
To forgive myself
To love myself

Grace
To make mistakes
To try again
To slowly grow

Permission
To dare
To dream
To simply be

Faith
Enough to believe
Enough to trust
Enough to not fear

Space
So I may spread my wings
So I may grow into my dreams
So I may exceed my limits

Discipline
Of habit
Of faith
Of mind

Peace
I seek stillness
I quiet the noise
I move at my pace

Love of self
It guides me
It heals me
It nourishes me.

Today I will live unfiltered
Aware of weaknesses, faults, and flaws
Allowing them to exist as pieces of me
I need not hide them

Today I will live unfiltered
Aware of the bruises, scars, and weathered pieces
Loving myself for having fought for them
I need not hide them

Today I will live unfiltered
Aware of the strengths I have gained
Quietly embracing them as I move forward
I need not hide them

Today I will live unfiltered
Aware of my own subtle hues of light
Letting them shine, if only for me
I need not hide them

Today I will live unfiltered
Aware of the curves and jagged edges
Finding within them my unique brand of beautiful
I need not hide them

Today I will live unfiltered
Aware that I need not hide.

Random thoughts, takeaways, and lessons on how living is like running a half-marathon:

1. In the difficult moments, it is about catching your breath, and yet never fearing the breathlessness.

2. The downhills were never intended to be easy; they are meant to build momentum for the uphills.

3. Joy and pain are not distant cousins, but rather fraternal twins. Each is meant to teach you how to handle the other.

4. It may look like it, but no one is dealing with the same task you've been given. Therefore, comparisons are of no relevance.

5. You can wish to do well or prepare to succeed. The latter eliminates the need for the former.

6. The challenge you face should never be addressed with the qualifier "just."

7. The prize is always ahead of you. Never behind you. Live forward.

8. If you are doing it, you are strong enough.

9. Fear and faith are both flames. One consumes. One fuels.

10. It may seem as though you are never going to arrive, and then you are there.

I recently concluded my twenty-eighth year of teaching middle school. I took a little time to reflect on some of the lessons I have learned along the way.

1. Being stuck in the middle, of anything, is rarely easy.

2. People change, grow, move on. Your job is to encourage them to do so.

3. You can raise your expectations without ever having to raise your voice.

4. The three most important Rs: routine, responsibility, respect. Set it. Expect it. Model it.

5. Even if the lesson does not go as planned, something is always learned.

6. What is tolerated becomes the norm. Be mindful of what you allow.

7. You do not always get to choose who comes into your space, but you always get to choose how you treat them.

8. The greatest of teachers have mastered the art of gentle persuasion.

9. The question they most want an answer to: Do you care about me?

10. The strongest bond is forged between teacher and pupil when both come to realize this: I can learn from you.

11. You cannot see into the future; you can only hope to positively influence it.

12. To teach is to empower. And the most powerful lesson you can teach: "I believe in you."

13. Holding their hand may give them comfort; letting go gives them wings.

14. If you desire another to climb beyond their fear, you must do one of two things: show them the net or be the net.

This is a science lesson.

You probably know by now that your body possesses a fight-or-flight response. It is a reaction to something that frightens you. Your body is put on high alert as a way of preparing you either to stay and deal with the threat or to flee to safety.

At numerous points in your life, you have experienced this response. Perhaps as you look ahead to what is waiting on the horizon, you are beginning to feel it well up inside again.

The elevated heartbeat as your body attempts to pump blood to the major muscle groups needed for the battle or the run. The dilated pupils as your body needs to allow more light to better view the threat or the path to safety. The activated sweat glands as your body attempts to keep itself cooled during the ensuing fight or impending miles. The rapid breathing as your body desperately tries to increase the flow of oxygen to your vital organs.

Add these all up, and your body is prepared to face the imminent danger or to lead you safely from it.

But here's the thing. Did you know your body responds the exact same way when you are excited, feeling joy, in love? The racing heartbeat. The googly eyes. The sweaty palms. The hyperventilating.

So questions remain. If your body has only one response, why does fear not feel like excitement? Why do panic and joy appear at opposite ends of the spectrum? Why is dread nothing at all like love?

The answer: it is how you and your brain have decided to label the trigger for this response.

So, right now, all the excitement you should be feeling? You have decided to call it fear. And it makes you want to run away from it. So, right now, all the joy you should be feeling? You have decided to mark it as panic. And it puts you in a frenzy. So, right now, all the love you should be inviting in? You have decided to attach dread to it. And it steals the most precious of all gifts.

Your body knows only one thing to do. And it will do it. You do not have a choice in that.

It is up to you to change the lens through which your mind views the situation.

Because between fear and excitement, between panic and joy, between dread and love, there exists a choice.

This is a life lesson.

Lessons I am still learning:

1. Things do not always go as planned, so I am learning to adjust accordingly, or to have a plan B, C, D, and E at the ready.

2. That which is tangible is rarely within my control, so I am learning to control my intangibles. Thoughts, effort, words, responses.

3. Fair does not mean equal, so I am learning not to compare what I receive or achieve to another. I do not expect equal; I expect what I work for. That seems fair.

4. Struggling and failing do not exist as a cause and effect, so I am learning my struggle did not lead to my failure. In reality, it prevented it.

5. The prerequisite for accomplishing the impossible is you must attempt the impossible, so I am learning to set my bar beyond my current capacity to reach. And I must keep trying.

6. External change is inevitable. It is called *weathering*. Internal change is optional. It is called *choice*. So I am learning to change my internals. Thoughts, effort, words, responses.

7. Today does not alter yesterday, but it has an influence on tomorrow, so I am learning to use today to launch myself in the direction I want to head tomorrow.

I am still learning, so I am learning to allow myself room for mistakes, growth, do-overs, and setbacks.

Lessons from a good, hard race:

1. Your hill always has another side, but you must first brave the climb.

2. Many will travel the course, yet no one will know your journey, so comparisons are invalid.

3. If something is beyond your ability to control, you should not invest energy trying to do so.

4. Your challenge, in the face of challenge, is to never give up hope.

5. Pain is mostly localized; it spreads when it becomes your sole focus.

6. Your mental capacity to endure far exceeds your physical limits; get your mind right.

7. The work you are doing is not intended to lessen the hurt, but to lessen your desire to quit when the hurt arrives.

8. What you most want will require you to endure the most.

9. Success resides in finding joy within your personal growth.

10. Everyone starts. Everyone finishes. The difference, then, is what you do with the time in between.

Lessons from a good, hard life.